Marriage á La Bombeck

Psychologists and marriage counselors say that the first year of marriage is the toughest because of the adjustments each one must make to the other. Couples do a lot of thinking.

From time to time, I thought of murder. I considered becoming Sister Erma Louise in St. Mary's convent. I even thought of going home to Mother's. (What for? He'd have been there in the kitchen having coffee with my parents.)

But divorce? Never.

On our first anniversary, which is symbolically paper, I lit a candle to illuminate two bowls of canned chili and he gave me my gift—a fishing license.

Maybe I spoke too soon.

❧   ❧   ❧

"Like the column she's known for, this book is full of laughs but also explores serious subjects."
—*USA Today*

"Bombeck's tale offers some of the best wisdom around." —*Alta Vista Magazine*

"Rife with her trademark wit."
—*Arizona Republic*

"Erma Bombeck is back, mining gems of domestic drollery. . . . Each chapter rattles a different funny bone." —*Cleveland Plain Dealer*

"Bombeck [is] one of America's favorite authors and humor columnists. When she writes about her life, readers see theirs."
—*Des Moines Register*

Books by Erma Bombeck

At Wit's End

"Just Wait Till You Have Children of Your Own!"

I Lost Everything in the Post-Natal Depression

The Grass Is Always Greener Over the Septic Tank

If Life Is a Bowl of Cherries, What Am I Doing in the Pits?

Aunt Erma's Cope Book

Motherhood: The Second Oldest Profession

Family: The Ties That Bind . . . and Gag!

*I Want to Grow Hair, I Want to Grow Up,
I Want to Go to Boise**

*When You Look Like Your Passport Photo,
It's Time to Go Home**

*A Marriage Made in Heaven . . .
Or Too Tired for an Affair**

***Published by
HarperPaperbacks**

HarperSpotlight

Erma Bombeck

A Marriage Made in Heaven . . . Or Too Tired for an Affair

HarperPaperbacks

A Division of HarperCollinsPublishers

HarperPaperbacks   *A Division of* HarperCollins*Publishers*
                    10 East 53rd Street, New York, N.Y. 10022

Copyright © 1993 by Erma Bombeck
All rights reserved. No part of this book may be used or reproduced in any manner whatsoever without written permission of the publisher, except in the case of brief quotations embodied in critical articles and reviews. For information address HarperCollins*Publishers*,
10 East 53rd Street, New York, N.Y. 10022.

A hardcover edition of this book was published in 1993 by HarperCollins*Publishers*.

Cover photograph © 1993 by Simon Metz

First HarperPaperbacks printing: November 1994

Printed in the United States of America

HarpcrPaperbacks, HarperSpotlight, and colophon are trademarks of HarperCollins*Publishers*

❖ 10 9 8 7 6 5 4 3 2 1

Contents

1949

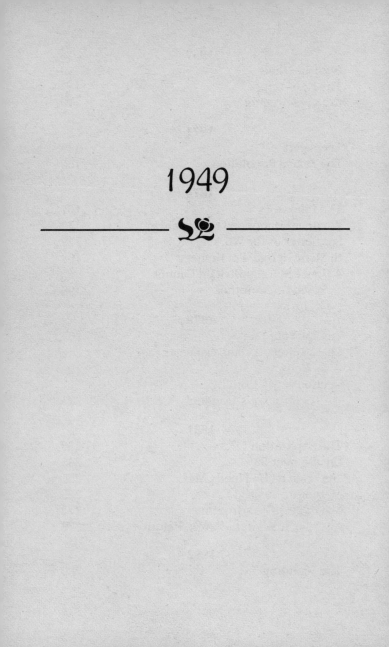

The Wedding

—— ❧ ——

It would have been a wonderful wedding—had it not been mine.

The sun was shining. Relatives were speaking to one another. The bridegroom showed up. At the altar waiting for me was a man I met in high school, who had served in Korea following World War II, and who looked great in a uniform. Ernest Borgnine looked great in a uniform!

Bill was a stranger. I had only known him for seven years. People had longer conversations with waiters over the "specials."

What could my parents be thinking of with all that drivel about "You're not getting any younger?" We had no car, no place to live, no furniture, and no sterling silver pattern. I wondered if you were legally married if you didn't have a sterling silver pattern. Bill didn't even have a job. He had a year left of college. No doubt about it. My parents were making a big mistake!

Nothing was working out right. As a child I had always fantasized about having a wedding that was above our means. And here I was in an oversized bridal gown that I bought on sale, a cousin snapping our wedding album pictures with a box camera, and my mom smelling like the baked ham she cooked all morning to transport to the wedding reception.

And what was going to happen to my dreams? I had big plans for me. On my graduation from college, I was going to New York to work for the *New York Times* as a foreign correspondent. If that fell through, I had a firm offer to write obituaries for the *Dayton Herald* in Ohio.

Now, here I was two weeks after my graduation, walking down the aisle of the Church of the Resurrection to say "I do" without so much as a job description.

I met the gaze of my bridegroom, who was waiting for me at the altar, and poverty

The Wedding

and unfulfilled dreams seemed unimportant. What was the matter with me? I loved the man. We were the perfect couple. We had everything in common. Well, the things that really mattered.

We both chewed only a half stick of gum and saved the other half. (How many people did that!) We both loved Robert Benchley's humor, hated communism, and what was the other thing? Oh yes, we both loathed going to the dentist. A lot of couples we knew started off their marriages with less.

As I knelt by his side, I observed through my veil that he had a smattering of white paint on his ear. The faint odor of turpentine hung over him. He painted houses in the summer for extra money. That would have to change. Surely, he could find something more dignified to do. Besides, I had no intention of hanging around someone with whom you're afraid to light a match.

The man definitely needed work. But I had years ahead to mold him into the husband he was capable of being. First, I made a mental note to let his hair grow out. God, I hated his burr. It made him look like a shag rug that had just been vacuumed.

And we'd have to do something about his eating habits. I came from a family that considered gravy a beverage. He ate vegetables, which I regarded as decorations for the mantel. Imagine spending the rest of your life with a man who had never had cold dumplings for breakfast!

His best man and poker-playing buddy, Ed Phillips, passed him the ring. I smiled as Bill slipped it on my finger. Ed and the entire group of merry little men were soon to be part of the past. No more single life—playing poker until all hours of the morning. From here on in, it would just be the two of us, watching sunsets and gazing into one another's eyes.

As our shoulders touched, I was challenged by the idea of setting up a schedule for him. All the years we had been dating, he had been late for everything. I was vowing to spend eternity with a man who had never heard the "Star-Spangled Banner" or seen a kickoff at a game . . . never watched a curtain go up or heard an overture. He looked so relaxed. He couldn't know that I would soon teach him the virtues of putting the cap on a ballpoint pen so that it wouldn't dry out and instruct him on how left-handed people are supposed to hang up the phone so they won't drive right-handed people crazy.

The priest was Polish and between his

The Wedding

accent and the Latin of the Mass, I strained to interpret his words. Then loud and clear I heard him admonish, "You, Bill, are to be the head of the house and you, Erma, are to be the heart."

In his dreams. What did he think he was dealing with here . . . a child who chose a nickel over a dime because it was bigger? I had seen the "heart detail" and I didn't struggle through four years of conjugating verbs to get choked up over my husband's high bowling scores.

Maybe I could talk Bill into being the heart . . . or at least trade off once in a while.

I now pronounce you man and wife.

With the possible exceptions of "We have lift-off" and "This country is at war," there are few phrases as sobering.

The reception was held in a social hall near the edge of town, usually reserved for VFW picnics. Folding chairs lined the wall, giving the hall the intimacy of a bus station. A long table covered with white paper was in the center of the room and held the cake and the mound of ham sandwiches.

A car pulled up to the entrance. A couple with six kids piled out. The man yelled to no one in particular, "Charlie's here! Where's the beer?"

Bill looked at me and asked, "Yours?"

I nodded. "My uncle by marriage."

The rest of the day was a blur—relatives lining up on opposite sides of the room like two warring tribes . . . hundreds of children no one had ever seen before with cake on their faces . . . bridesmaids giving you that "Thank God it's you and not me" look . . . and Mother, who couldn't stop crying because she was running out of ham.

A well-wisher asked where we were going on our honeymoon. I told her I wanted to go to New York City and see a Broadway show and stay at a fancy hotel and ride in a carriage at midnight through Central Park.

"So, where are you going?" she pressed.

"We're going fishing at Larvae Lake in Michigan."

"You married romance," she smiled.

What could I expect from a man who proposed by sliding my engagement ring over his cigar and lighting it?

At around four o'clock, I looked for Bill. He was nowhere to be found. Outside in the parking lot, I spotted him with Ed and the whole gang of his buddies laughing and drinking beer and setting up a poker game to begin the moment he got back.

It was going to be harder than I thought.

Living on Love

***

The adjustment we all feared and never talked about was sex. In the '40s, few of my friends had had undress rehearsals. Besides, we all figured anything the Catholic Church encouraged—like marital sex—couldn't be much fun.

The biggest problem with sex was working it into our busy schedules. Sex between two and three on Saturdays was out of the question because the paperboy collected then. Before breakfast was out because we always overslept. Forget after dinner. One of our parents always called and if we didn't answer our phone, they called the police.

Tuesday was bowling night and Bill got home late, and Fridays I always washed my hair and slept in curlers so it would "set," so forget Fridays.

One night at card club, one of my friends quoted an article she had read that claimed the thrill of sex wears off after two years of marriage.

When we tried to figure out what would replace it, the answers ranged from hot fudge sundaes to gum surgery.

Adjustment to sex wasn't even in the top ten.

The real problems were ones we hadn't counted on. Newlyweds should forget all that garbage about cherishing and loving one another for better or for worse, for richer or for poorer, in sickness and in health, and address the big question, "Can you feed and maintain yourselves?" You'd think someone would tell you when you are embarking on a sea of matrimony—pack a lunch!

When I was single and shallow, I vaguely remember my mother saying to me one night, "While you are up, would you get me a glass of water from the kitchen?"

I asked, "Where is it?"

She said, "Which one is a problem for you? The water or the kitchen?"

Living on Love

"The kitchen," I answered.

"It's the room with the big clock in it."

"Oh."

From time to time when I lived at home, she had tried to get me to observe her at work in the kitchen, but I had no curiosity as to how an egg got out of the shell or how chickens got dressed. At twenty-two, I still believed aspic was a ski resort.

I had taken a few home economics classes in high school, but it was only a matter of time before the steady diet of white sauce and divinity fudge made us mean.

Bill put down his fork over his uneaten mystery meal one night and said, "Maybe we should take back some of these wedding gifts and exchange them for something useful."

"Like what?"

"Vending machines."

The reality was, we were discovering the meaning of life was food. During the dating process, we had lived on love, which has no calories, no nutritional value, and requires very little preparation time.

Now we were discovering that not only was our next meal the reason for our existence, it was the basis of all of our communication.

"What are we having for dinner?"

"What do you want me to fix?"

"Did you get to the store?"

"Did you unthaw it?"

"Is this the way your mother cooks it?"

"Is it too tough?"

"Is it too done?"

"Is that cut too expensive?"

"Do you want me to save this?"

"You're not eating."

If we weren't discussing our eating habits, my mother was calling to find out what I was having for dinner or my in-laws checked in to see if their son was taking nourishment.

Neither of us wanted to admit it, but the meals we mooched each week from our respective parents were IV lifelines. They had replaced our umbilical cords.

We had entered marriage and brought along all the wrong things. Why I thought I needed silver place-card holders in my "hope chest," I'll never know. Everyone knew you didn't need ID at my dinner table. You wouldn't stay long enough to make friends.

The wedding gifts had been no help whatsoever. Well-meaning friends had given us little trivets shaped like eagles. We needed a bathroom heater. We had iced tea spoons. We needed a mattress for the bed. We were recipients of two living room lamps. We needed tables to put them on.

Living on Love

Our apartment looked like someone had crocheted it . . . thanks to my Aunt Mae. When she heard I was getting married, she crocheted herself into a coma. There was a crocheted cover for our toilet tank and seat, a contour rug, an oval rug for use in front of the bowl, a cover for the toilet tissue, and a tieback for the shower curtain.

There were also crocheted covers for the bar of soap, the nose tissue, cleanser can, facial tissue, and a little hat to decorate the wall.

She had left nothing undressed in the entire apartment. There was a Mexican serape and ten-gallon hat over our Tabasco sauce and a bottle of wine dressed as a poodle. She had made a costume for every doorknob in our house, plus doilies for the backs and arms of every chair, an afghan to drape on the footstool, and sets of coasters and throws for the tables that we didn't have.

If I didn't win any prizes in the kitchen, Bill certainly didn't shine as a handyman.

"Maybe we could exchange some of these wedding gifts for a hammer," I suggested one day.

"What for?" he asked sharply.

"For things like putting up a mailbox and a towel rack in the bathroom."

"I never told you I was handy," he said defensively.

"I'm not talking heavy machinery that you can't use after taking a cold capsule. I'm talking about a hammer."

"My dad had one of those in the basement," he mused.

"It might be fun for you to get a little drill and maybe a screwdriver. Who knows, someday you could—"

"Wait a minute," he interrupted. "We're back to Tom and Jeanne's Ping-Pong ball clock again, aren't we? This is what this conversation is all about."

Tom and Jeanne are good friends who were married three weeks before us. Their apartment was to die for. The walls were painted deep green. They had bought old furniture and refinished it in white and yellow. They framed posters, and Jeanne had made dried flower arrangements that hung in the kitchen. Tom had made a lamp out of stacked flower pots, and together they fashioned bookshelves out of cement blocks and planks. But the eye-catcher was Tom's clock. He had taken the innards of an old clock and around them had fashioned a stunning timepiece using painted Ping-Pong balls attached to small wooden dowels.

Living on Love

"There's nothing wrong with our apartment," he said defensively.

"It has the warmth of a recovery room."

"I've done some things," he said.

"Lining the shelves with ConTac paper and sticking a nail over the sink to hold unpaid bills does not exactly make a decorating statement."

The biggest problem was that we were poor and totally unprepared for marriage. To tell you the truth, I thought it was going to be more fun than it was. Our parents had talked about their struggle through the lean years with so much enthusiasm and laughter, it made us sick we missed the Depression.

Occasionally, I allowed myself to think of the promise I had made to myself at the altar—to create a husband who would be totally compatible.

There had been no progress there either. It was very discouraging. He still had the burr haircut. He continued to hang out with Ed and the guys. And he was still late for everything. A forty-four-minute egg for breakfast had become a way of life.

What was more discouraging is that I was adding daily to the list of things that needed fixing on him.

He was a night person and I was a day

person. He walked into walls until noon. When I was ready to go to bed, he was getting his second wind.

He didn't tan. You'd have thought in the seven years I dated him that he would have said he hated the beach and his Irish skin could not tolerate daylight.

He left his entire wardrobe in his closet regardless of whether it was winter or summer. How could you live like that, with seersuckers and wools side by side? And—this may seem like a small thing, but stay with me—if there were two boxes of cereal half full, he combined them. Same with ice cream and juices, so you never really knew what you were eating.

Not only that, I discovered the man was incapable of putting a toilet seat lid down.

But possibly the biggest adjustment was the Tuesday Night Experience.

We promised ourselves our marriage would never fall into a rut. Yet, here we were every Tuesday night of our lives participating in a ritual second only to the pageantry and predictability of the Changing of the Guard at Buckingham Palace: dinner at his parents.

They were nice people, but I was totally intimidated by them. His mother stayed at home and wore hose all day; mine worked in a factory and wore slacks. Their house had a dining room and a china closet. My family ate in the kitchen where you could sit at the table and turn off the stove and open the refrigerator without moving. They were a good twenty years older than my parents.

As a concession to me, we timed our visits with *The Milton Berle Show.* (They also owned a television set!) As we entered the house we could hear, "Oh we're the men from Texaco . . . we come from Maine to Mexico. . . ." Within minutes, two things would happen. Milton Berle would prance before his audience on the sides of his shoes and Mother Bombeck would give her son the only vegetable he had seen since last Tuesday.

I felt like Eliza Doolittle eating for the first time at the table of Professor Henry Higgins . . . and living for the day when they would nod at one another and say, "She's got it. I think she's got it."

At my family's house, my father didn't lose a daughter; he gained a closet and a son-in-law who got stuck with my dry cleaning bills. My mother, who had vowed at the wedding that the man I was marrying was "not good enough" for me, now turned on me and said, "He's worth two of you."

Erma Bombeck

She couldn't heap enough praise on her new "son." He would bring her a pitiful bouquet of flowers and she'd say, "Erma never got me flowers you didn't have to dust before." She felt sorry for my husband because he "looked thin," wasn't being fed properly, and because he had worn pink underwear for a month when a red towel faded in the laundry. In short, she loved him.

Psychologists and marriage counselors say that the first year of marriage is the toughest because of the adjustments each one must make to the other. Couples do a lot of thinking.

From time to time, I thought of murder. I considered becoming Sister Erma Louise in St. Mary's convent. I even thought of going home to Mother's. (What for? He'd have been there in the kitchen having coffee with my parents.)

But divorce? Never.

We had something going here. He had nailed two cigar boxes together, painted them yellow (King Edward was bleeding through) and called them decorative shadow boxes. I had bought a cookbook for the domestically impaired. We scraped together $150 to buy a twelve-year-old Plymouth. One Tuesday, I had a cold and we didn't go to his family's house for dinner.

Living on Love

On our first anniversary, which is symbolically paper, I lit a candle to illuminate two bowls of canned chili and he gave me my gift—a fishing license.

Maybe I spoke too soon.

"We Interrupt This Marriage . . ."

✦

She wasn't all that attractive. She was small, colorless, and came with a little history—but she knew how to play a male audience and turned men's heads wherever she went.

I knew the moment Bill brought her home, placed her on a pedestal table, and positioned himself on a vanity bench two feet in front of her that our marriage would never be the same again.

A television set in our house was like sleeping three in a bed. I personally found the appliance whining, demanding, possessive, and shallow, but to Bill she was the perfect companion. If he snored, it didn't matter. If he fell asleep in the middle of her conversation, she forgave him. If he demanded she light up in the middle of the night and entertain him, she was glad to do it. He could turn her on by pushing a button and dismiss her whenever he felt like it.

The impact of television on marriage was awesome. There wasn't a woman who wasn't threatened by it. Meals were planned around it. Social life revolved around its schedules. Sex was worked in around the commercial breaks. But mostly, our lives were shaped by its contents.

My contemporaries and I got a weekly diet of women who wore hose and pearls all day long and never scrubbed a toilet bowl and men who came home, scratched the dog behind the ear, pecked their wives on the cheek (or was it the other way around), and changed into a jacket with patches on the elbows.

But mostly, television for women— especially the commercials—defined and reinforced our roles.

The message was we alone bore the responsibility for the success or failure of our husbands. If we didn't feed him a rib-sticking warm breakfast, he would develop irregularities and lose clients. If his bath towel was scratchy, he would be irritable in the workplace. And God forbid the boss would come to dinner and the glasses were spotted or streaked. He'd never get that promotion and it would be our fault.

Even men began to believe it. One day Bill approached me with his shirt and sang tauntingly, "Honey, ring around the collar."

"So why don't you wash your crummy neck!" I snapped.

I wanted to believe the daily lives of the couples on the soaps . . . the men who sat around the kitchen all day long and said to their wives, "Do you want to talk about it, Joanne?" In real life, our conversation had been reduced to about six words a week. We didn't even argue anymore. By the time there was a break in *Ozzie and Harriet* or Sid Caesar's *Your Show of Shows,* we forgot what it was we were going to argue about. I found myself envying Fran . . . at least she had two puppets, Kukla and Ollie, to talk with.

Most of the time, however, Bill was with his electronic "mistress." He was sitting on the 50-yard line or under every basket, following every hockey puck, serving at the net, catching behind home plate, and shouting at ringside.

I could have appeared in a nightgown made out of Astroturf and a number on my back and he would have sat with his eyes glued to the set and asked, "We out of dip?"

I was a fool for trying to get his attention. Years later, I remember seeing Suzanne Pleshette on *The Tonight Show* with Johnny Carson. There she sat, her curves straining to escape a long black crepe dress. Her alabaster skin took your breath away and rows of white teeth smiled seductively. She was complaining she couldn't get her husband away from the television tube and football for five minutes. If Suzanne Pleshette couldn't hold her husband's attention, what chance did I have?

I knew in my heart if we ever had children, they'd all talk like Howard Cosell. Bill wasn't just a spectator, he was a *sleeptator*.

Spectators cheer. They jump out of their chairs occasionally. They take nourishment (sometimes intravenously). Their eyes blink. But the *sleeptator* just sits there in front of the television set with his eyes closed. For all purposes, he is somewhere between the fourth quarter and death.

Enter the spouse, who truly believes her husband is asleep. She reaches over to turn off the monotone drone of the announcer when the lump speaks. "Touch that dial and you're a dead woman."

Erma Bombeck

What really amazed me was the buildup Bill gave to every event. It's all he talked about. An hour before the game began he would position his chair in front of the set, line up his snacks and his cooler, and take the phone off the hook. Minutes before, he visited the bathroom. Right after the kickoff, he sank into a coma.

As a newlywed, it's hard to face up to the fact that you can be replaced by a talking horse. But it was true. If we ever had a family, it would have to be conceived on a vanity bench during a razor blade commercial.

At Christmastime, I hung tinsel from his ears and tried to make him look festive. When we had company, I had them write three questions for him to answer before they got there. At one point, my mother expressed concern that we might have to hook him up to a catheter.

But the seduction that we wives had all hoped was a harmless little diversion in our marriage was here to stay. Even on Saturday nights when we visited one another's small apartments, the men would hover around the tube in the living room and the women would be off in the kitchen by themselves asking the big question, "What happened to our marriages?"

"We Interrupt This Marriage . . ."

One night, we were all sitting around trying to find a solution for our loneliness. Joan was relating a spellbinding commercial where a woman had used an inferior home permanent that gave her dull, lifeless hair with the result that her husband preferred work to coming home—when a man entered the kitchen.

None of us knew him. We figured he got lost on his way back from the bathroom and said, "The men are in the living room listening to Howard Cosell."

"Howard who?" he asked.

We looked at him in disbelief. "You're kidding. You mean you really have never heard of Howard Cosell?" He shook his head.

"How about the Dolphins?" asked Helen, her eyes narrowing with suspicion.

"I saw them in Miami."

Our hopes fell.

"They have a great Seaquarium there," he added.

"What's your name?" I said, edging closer.

"Bob."

"Tell me, Bob," I said, "what do you do on New Year's Day?"

"Change the water in my water bed and have a late supper."

"And all day Sunday?"

"Take a drive in the country, catch a movie somewhere in the evening."

No one breathed.

"And what about Monday?" asked Charmaine.

"Stay at home, listen to records. Visit with someone."

We couldn't believe it. We were in a room with a man who didn't care about sports or television.

I still had to be convinced.

"When we throw a word at you," I said, "answer quickly the first thing that comes to mind. Quarterback!"

"What you find in a recliner chair after a cheap friend has sat in it."

"Oklahoma."

"Rodgers and Hammerstein."

"O.J."

"Orange juice and Anita Bryant."

It was the only neighborhood party Bob ever attended, but there wasn't a day we didn't mention his name.

In 1953, television brought two major events into our living room. The New York Yankees won the World Series again and Lucille Ball actually became pregnant, giving birth to TV son little Ricky, as millions of viewers tuned in.

"We Interrupt This Marriage . . ."

I had seen pregnancies on the soaps before, but the expectant mothers walked around with stomachs no bigger than someone who had eaten a big lunch and usually miscarried so they wouldn't get stuck with boring plots or have to pay scale for the kid to talk.

But Lucy was for real . . . on and off screen.

She and Ethel had romped through a candy factory, stomped grapes together, and Lucy had set fire to her nose in front of William Holden. Now it was time for her to move on to motherhood.

As I watched the bungling quartet running around the apartment bumping into doors, grabbing the wrong suitcase in a frenzy to get Lucy to the hospital, only one question haunted me: How did she ever get Desi away from the TV set long enough to make a baby?

In Sickness and in Health

❧❧

Some people are born to be pillow fluffers and soup pushers. Their touch can bring temperatures down to normal. They can run and fetch with the loyalty of a cocker spaniel. To a sick person, it's like being in the hands of Allstate.

Other people regard illness as an annoying news bulletin during the Super Bowl or a numbness like when your parents come home early when you're throwing a party.

Mixed marriages between a sympathizer and an intolerant are not uncommon. Compassion is not necessarily a gender thing. Normally, one mate will take and the other will give.

In Sickness and in Health

In our marriage, neither of us liked to watch people throw up. We didn't know how to deal with our own illnesses—let alone anyone else's. It was something our mothers had always done for us.

If I announced that my eyes felt like round razor blades, my throat was parched, my lips were cracked, and I was burning with fever and I wanted my husband to remarry when I was gone, he would look at me and say, "Let me get this straight. What you are really saying is that you want me to pick up the cleaning."

I was no better. If I suggested he see a doctor and he turned macho-martyr on me, I'd say, "Fine, you are going to die. Just tell me what weight of motor oil you use in the car before you go."

Instead of heaping love and concern on one another, we both tended to indemnify ourselves of any blame for the illness. He would say, "Well, you finally got your cold, didn't you?" (Like I shopped for it).

I don't know if it was the stress of being married or if my warranties were expiring. Whatever it was, during the first few years of wedded bliss, we discovered I was put together like a cheap Japanese watch.

First, it was my tonsils.

"You mean you still have them?" asked my husband.

"What do you think I do? Grow them? Of course I still have them and they have to come out."

"You are going to be the oldest person in the pediatric ward."

A month or so later, I came down with the mumps.

My cheeks were so heavy we tied them up with a large bandanna.

Bill wasn't as compassionate as he was puzzled. "Why would you wait until you were married to have mumps?"

"I thought it would make the time go faster," I said icily.

By the time I got the word from my dentist that my teeth had to be straightened, his patience was running out.

"People like you should come with a warranty," he said.

"And people like you don't deserve a wife. You should have married a toaster!"

"All I know," he countered, "is that you need more repairs than our '38 Plymouth."

A few months later when I landed in the hospital with a kidney infection, I overheard Bill telling my father, "I have to take my hat off to you. You sure knew when to unload her."

In Sickness and in Health

My dad just smiled. "Look upon it as an investment, Son."

The first serious illness we had to face occurred one day when Bill decided to install a humidifier. I personally would not have tried to install a 900-pound piece of equipment lying flat on my back and pushing it with my feet, but there are some people who won't listen.

As I stood over his body, which lay flat on the floor like a welcome mat, I said, "I knew you wouldn't rest until you slipped a disk."

The major problem with a bad back is that it's as common as dirt. Everyone either has one, had one, is going to have one, knew someone who had one, or took someone to lunch who has one.

The second major problem is that everyone has a cure to make it go away.

Sleep with a teddy bear between your knees.

Sleep on a vibrating bed of river rock.

Have a member of your family sneak up behind you and surprise you with the Heimlich maneuver.

Go to this great doctor who unfortunately died two years ago.

Bill's doctor recommended traction. I rented a harness to buckle up around his

Erma Bombeck

hips and attached the pulleys to two Super
Kem-Tone paint cans filled with cement that
dangled over the foot of the bed.

"Are you going to be all right?" I asked as
I pulled a sweater out of the closet.

"Why?" he moaned.

"Because I'm off to the mall. If you have
to go to the bathroom, tell me now."

I cared about him. It's just that people
who strain their backs are never doing anything to benefit mankind when they do it. It is
always triggered by something stupid like lift-
ing a car or the corner of a building or something equally dumb.

Being sensitive to one another's needs is
not easy. A few years after Bill's bout with a
slipped disk, I lifted a rather large flower pot
one day. Two days later, I said to him as he
passed the bedroom door, "Hi there. Did I
ever tell you how bad I felt for you when you
had your disk problem?"

"No," he said.

"I really felt terrible. You seemed to be so
helpless and I know you were in a lot of
pain."

"Why are you bringing this up now?" he
asked cautiously.

"Because I can't lift the toilet seat lid. I
hate to ask, but while you're bent down,

could you possibly get my glasses and turn over my bedroom slipper that's on its back?"

"Did I tell you? Man was never meant to walk upright."

"I haven't walked upright in two days," I said. "You didn't notice me crawling under the table in the kitchen?"

"Everyone has back problems," he said. "It's like the common cold."

"Except mine is different," I said. "It's hard to describe, but I'll try. You know how a toaster looks when it clicks off and is cooling down and the heat just sorta keeps sliding down on all those little coils?"

He stared at me without speaking.

"Other times it's not burning so much as it is a dull pain. You know like you're sitting at an Ohio State football game on a cold, hard bleacher for three hours and it's ten degrees below and you look around for someone who can carry you to the car in that chair-locked position because there isn't a way in this world you can stand?"

"I get the idea," he said.

"No, wait! You know what's it's like to roll over on a pit bull that you startle out of a sound sleep? That's it!"

As we moved from one malady to another during our marriage, we seemed to get a handle on what was expected of us. All he wanted from me was his prescription filled and a dark room with the door shut. When I was on my back, I could expect to be served the only dish he cooked . . . a plate of fried potatoes and onions, stirred with a paring knife, with a peanut butter and banana sandwich on the side.

Over the years, we got rather good at comforting one another. Illness has to be one of the tests of a marriage. That's why they put it in the marriage vows. Everyone sorta glides over it, but it's important. For the first time, you are caught naked with your pretenses down. (Not to mention makeupless.) You are vulnerable and you are dependent. Neither of you married to have the other partner "take care of you." You were supposed to be a team. And now you are being seen in a compromising scene with your head hung into a toilet bowl at 2 A.M. while another person stands over you, taking away any shred of modesty or mystique you have left.

My friends, who had babies, said that not only would I develop compassion after I had my first child, I would say good-bye to modesty. They told stories of how they had entered the hospital with weights in the hems of their maternity tops and requested two sheets at the gynecologist's office.

After they delivered, all that changed. A stream of men they had never seen before whipped in and out of their hospital rooms like they were whirling in revolving doors. Male doctors surveyed their bare chests with stethoscopes and threw back the sheets to "take a look at what we have here." They thumped, probed, squeezed, and pushed on every part of their bodies. They interrupted their baths to inquire about their irregularities and watched them struggle with hospital gowns that were too small to set a cocktail glass on.

I didn't believe any of this.

Of course that was before I delivered my first child and bared my bosom to a doctor in the hall to ask, "I'm nursing. Does this look normal to you?" only to have a nurse tell me he was a telephone repairman.

1953

"You Aren't Getting Any Younger"

❧❧

I put down the stubby pencil, took a sip of the warm punch balanced on my knees, and waited for the rest of the group to finish writing.

Another confetti-filled evening at a baby shower with the same people. It seemed like only yesterday that I attended bridal parties where we sat around on folding chairs dressing clothespins in crepe paper and hyperventilating when we won a spatula.

My eyes rested on what I had written . . . a list of fourteen words had been formed out of the letters of the word BASSINET. Two of the words were dirty, but I'd still probably win the prize. Okay, so the skill wasn't something you put on your résumé, but it was pretty impressive at a shower. God knows, I had been to enough of them in the past four years. There wasn't a week went by without another one of my friends announcing that a baby was on the way. Pregnancy was an epidemic.

I watched the rest of the women in the room in silence as they feverishly chewed on their nails, straining for yet another word before the time was up. They anguished like they were on the verge of discovering the meaning of life.

The format at these things was predictable. If the pregnant mother-to-be opened your present first, that meant you were going to have the next baby. It didn't matter if the gift was from her ninety-three-year-old grandmother; the woman was stuck with giving birth and that was her problem.

Another guest was assigned to take down the expectant mother's remarks when she opened a gift. These were read back to her as comments she purportedly made on the night she conceived. (The humor of a squeal followed by, "It's wonderful, but it's so little," did not escape us.)

Absently, I gathered the ribbons that covered the floor and began tying them together to be passed around in a circle throughout

"You Aren't Getting Any Younger"

the room. Each one who got a knot would go into maternity clothes within the hour.

I was living proof that all this nonsense was neither scientific nor foolproof. I had had a million knots pass through my hands and here I was twenty-six years old and still childless. After four years of marriage, I had never had heartburn or morning sickness, never worn underwear with a drawstring, never had a baby throw up in my face, or caught my engagement ring in a stretch mark. Why was God punishing me?

My mother, who chanted a mantra in my ear for two years of "You don't need a baby," was now humming the old favorite, "You aren't getting any younger."

My mother-in-law said, "You can't be a career girl forever." (Right. Like writing obituaries would get me a *Time* cover.)

Our friends were a little less subtle. "What are you waiting for?"

In my grade-school health class, our teacher, Miss Riegel, made getting pregnant sound like a piece of cake. You so much as touched the same kernel of popcorn in the movie with a young man and bingo! you were pregnant.

It wasn't that way at all. No one worked harder at it. We followed every bit of advice that came our way.

Keep temperature charts.

Eat oysters.

Keep your hips elevated.

Relax.

Face the head of your bed toward Bethlehem.

Go in debt over your head.

Bill and I were ready for Door Number Three of our marriage. We already had opened Door Number One—a teaching job for him in a rural school. He had to teach everything from girls' Phys. Ed. to Holistic Car Repair, but it was good.

Door Number Two was a thirteen-year-old Plymouth that at least gave us wheels and, on the months with R in them, actually ran. Now we needed a family to complete our Christmas card.

We didn't talk openly about the problem. Neither wanted the other to feel guilty for what was not happening. Bill was a little more honest. Whenever he heard friends were expecting, he'd tell them how lucky they were and how he envied them. Me? I acted like I was glad it was them and not me. Sometimes I even set a glass on a friend's stomach and snapped, "So sorry, dear, I thought you were a mantel."

I resented the people who said, "Be

patient." I didn't want to deliver the first baby funded by Medicare. I wanted my baby now, while all my friends were having theirs.

On the worst days, I imagined what it would be like to go through life without children. With a two-income family, we would move into a stately mansion and buy flashy cars. I would become a wildly successful author and appear on talk shows and in magazines. I would be the only one in the neighborhood who owned a white suit and had wall-to-wall white carpeting throughout the house. Bill and I would travel around the world and possibly eat at the White House. What kind of life is that? We would come home to an empty house with nothing but a surly cat who crouched on top of the TV set looking mean at us because we had her altered—we were too busy for kittens.

We were a couple clearly off their timetable. Everyone knows marriage is like a train that makes intermittent stops at children, new house, new job, new car, and cruises, just to keep the trip interesting.

In four years, our train hadn't even slowed down at any of those places. It was stuck at tedium, boredom, meat loaf, and days that all looked alike.

Bill taught school all day and I wrote

obituaries. At night, we graded spelling papers for two classes of seventh graders who misspelled their own names.

We decided to adopt a child. Enter Miss Eberts, a social worker who told us our home and our lifestyle would undergo close scrutiny, but we should have a child in our home within two years.

Two years! That's the best they could do for a woman who had had hundreds of knots pass through her fingers at baby showers? And then Miss Eberts made a big mistake. She said, "Look, if it will make the time go faster for you, you can check in with me from time to time to see how it's going."

By the end of the week I had called Miss Eberts three times to ask her how it was going. In fact, I called her every week of our lives for two years. She could have run her life using my calls as a time frame. "Let's see, Erma called yesterday. My six-weeks dental checkup must be tomorrow." In short, I drove Miss Eberts nuts!

Bill said he had a vision of Miss Eberts hiding behind filing cabinets and standing on a seat in a restroom stall with her staff calling, "It's Mrs. Bombeck on the phone. Are you here?"

During the two-year waiting period there

were surprise home visitations. Ours occurred one Saturday when Bill was suffering from a case of poison oak on his legs. Miss Eberts arrived to see Bill with his foot in a beer cooler filled with a soaking solution. He held a beer can in his hand while he watched a football game. I was in grub clothes trying to make a room divider out of pink plastic clothesline by hooking it to the ceiling and weighting it down with rocks in a planter.

How did Ma and Pa Kettle explain you caught them at a bad time?

I offered Miss Eberts a cookie and a glass of iced tea. That the beverage was served in an old-fashioned glass escaped no one.

By the time they gave us a baby, I'd be too old to feed myself.

1954-1958

Children

--- 🌹 ---

Wanda and Dwayne didn't live in a house.
They lived in the Twilight Zone. Since the
birth of little Martin they just weren't the
same people.

Their house went from an orderly, warm,
personal reflection of two young people in
love to the decor of a penal institution.
Knobs had been removed from all the doors,
cupboards were wired shut, and a gate was
stretched at the top of the steps leading to
their basement. Tape covered all the recepta-
cles, mobiles dangled from the ceiling like icy
stalactites forcing you to crawl to the sofa.
You couldn't walk or sit down without some-

thing squeaking or playing a nursery rhyme.

Everything had been cleared out of the living room to make room for a giant playpen, rocking horses, small cars, and giant inflatable toys. The couple hadn't seen anything made of glass since Martin took his first step.

A potty seat in the bathroom played "The Impossible Dream" when you sat on it, and if you were fool enough to wonder what was being stored in a large pail near the toilet and removed the lid, you lost your vision for three-quarters of an hour. There was an odor to the house of strained lamb and talcum powder.

But it was Wanda and Dwayne we worried about. They were incapable of completing sentences anymore. Wanda would say, "Honey, did you . . . ?" and Dwayne would answer, "It's heating up." He would say, "I can't find . . . " and Wanda would answer, "It's on the top shelf in the hall closet."

Wanda schlepped around in bedroom slippers, and God only knows what she was hiding under her husband's oversized shirt, which she wore over slacks. I didn't even want to guess when was the last time she moisturized. Both seemed oblivious that their marriage was self-destructing before their eyes.

Children

They never went anywhere anymore. They seemed content to stay home and watch little Martin lie on his back in the middle of the living room, kicking his feet and screaming when he was denied anything. They beamed when he guzzled and slobbered in their guests' drinks. One night when he dumped the contents of my purse in the middle of the floor, Wanda yelled, "Oh Dwayne, get the camera, quick!"

Every time we visited them, Bill and I made a solemn vow that if we ever had children, we were not going to let them intrude into our marriage like little Martin did in Wanda and Dwayne's. We were never going to get so busy that we didn't banish the kids to their rooms and have some private time together ... especially at dinner. We were never going to get crazy enough to think that people wanted to sit around and wait for our child to burp. And we would never, repeat NEVER, put our fine things—assuming we got anything finer than Bill's bowling trophy—near the ceiling out of their reach. We would simply say, "Don't touch that or you will never see another Oreo cookie as long as you live" and that would be the end of it.

That's what we said.

We said that until just after the New Year

in 1954, when Miss Eberts from the adoption agency placed a seven-month-old, blue-eyed little girl in our arms with instructions to "be happy." We called her Betsy.

During the waiting period, my friends said I had the best of all worlds: no heartburn, no stomach to rearrange under a steering wheel, no water breaking in the middle of the night. Just open a package, add formula, stir with love, and voilà! you're a mother.

I remember thinking I also got cheated. I didn't experience that heart-stopping moment when the doctor would tell me, "You're pregnant." I missed the wondrous moment new parents go through the first time a baby moves inside you and together with your husband you cover your stomach with hands waiting for it to happen again. And I wondered wistfully what a baby from the two of us genetically would look like.

All of that was a bunch of garbage I told myself and others to make people think I also had suffered.

But none of it mattered when this child entered our lives. For the first time, we felt complete. Our lives took on a purpose we never had before. Half of our friends said she looked like me; the other half said she looked like Bill. The adjustment period took possibly ten minutes.

Within a week of her arrival, we made Wanda and Dwayne look like negligent parents. We were like two wild people rummaging through garbage cans at 2 A.M. looking for the pacifier, holding a mirror in front of her nose during the night to see if she was still breathing, and decorating the house in Early FAO Schwarz.

We called the pediatrician at any hour of the night to report a gas bubble. Visitors had to stand outside and watch her in the window from the front yard. It was like keeping vigil to see the Pope. Volume I of the baby book was filled at the end of the first month.

As we fell into bed each night exhausted, we both agreed she was a wondrous miracle. This had to be the best time of our lives.

Anyone who thinks that after a child invades your space you might emerge the same people you were before is naive. Our priorities were rearranged, our schedules obliterated. The woman who had dreams of working for the *New York Times* didn't have time to read a newspaper. The man who had to be awakened with a wrecking ball over his bed now jumped out of bed when he heard a hiccup from the nursery.

Slowly the focus of our existence shifted; it was no longer one another. We succumbed to the manger mentality that consumes all new parents.

The lines were drawn early for who did what. Bill was the daddy, and his job was to go out into the real world each day and work to bring strained squash to the table, and, as the mother, I was in charge of the house and everything in it.

But something bothered me. My hours were getting longer and my job description kept growing. Finally, one night as I fell back into bed totally wiped out, I said, "Why don't we split this wondrous miracle between us?"

"What are you talking about?" he said sleepily.

"What part of the baby do you want? The top or the bottom?"

"You can't separate a baby!"

"Of course you can," I yawned. "Do you want the top part that you have to feed every three hours or the bottom that has to be changed every three minutes?"

"You're serious, aren't you?" he said.

"Dead."

"Okay," he said reluctantly, "the top, but only when I'm home."

Actually, I didn't get such a bad deal out

of it. Oh sure, I got all the leaky plumbing and the legs that took off every chance they got, but he got the part that spit food back in his face whenever it was not to her liking, the Tooth Fairy bills for all the teeth that fell out, the oatmeal in the hair, the cussing, the "Why Daddy's?," the throwing up in the middle of the night, and random long-distance phone calls she placed.

The three of us were never on the same time cycle. When Bill and I were on work, shop, cook, and run, she was on perma-sleep and off. When we were asleep and exhausted, she was on spin-around-the-crib, damp, dry, and fill.

Our every waking hour was spent sterilizing, heating, changing, scrubbing, burping, rocking, and running. It was to be our destiny, and we were committed to it.

When we finally decided to take her to Mother's one Sunday for dinner, it looked like a Hemingway safari. The car was loaded with a playpen, perambulator, potty seat, and feeding table. Boxes were loaded with cotton balls, diapers, powders, lotions, teethers, toys, pacifiers, sterilizers, bottles, baby food, night lights, blankets, wardrobe changes, and a small reference library.

What Bill and I looked like and how we

were living didn't seem to matter anymore. The impact was driven home one afternoon when I realized there was nothing of either of us left in the house anymore. Our hobbies and our interests had been relegated to cardboard boxes and stored in the attic. Our favorite books had been replaced by Doctors Spock and Seuss. We didn't have toys of our own, like a tennis racket or golf clubs, anymore. They were replaced by head-bumping mobiles and shin-cracking rocking horses. Even our wedding picture had been replaced by a framed naked baby.

What had happened to those two young people who used to pop corn and play Scrabble and nibble on one another's ears? They were in the bathroom applauding bowel movements, that's where.

I had elevated exhaustion to state of the art. Had I been able to afford it, I would have hired someone to chew my food for me. But being the perennial optimist, I speculated that child-raising was a short-term proposition.

Give it a year or two and the kid would sleep through the night, open her own doors, amuse herself, and with the way things were going, mix her own formula and heat up her own bottle. If I had to arrange for a pacifier transplant, so be it.

Children

Then Bill and I could get back to our marriage, which had at the moment all the warmth of two people working together on a project for a science fair.

When I shared these thoughts that my job would end in a year or two with my mother, she smiled one of those maniacal little smiles that I had learned to dread.

"We'll see," she said.

I was worried. The last time she said that was when someone said we would never enter World War II.

How Much Happiness Can We Finance?

———— ❧ ————

The first wondrous miracle was thirteen months old when I discovered I was pregnant. Don't ask me how it happened. The doctors who said I would never conceive a child were either wrong or I was retaining more water than Hoover Dam.

The adoptive period of waiting was mentally stressful. But my friends were right. It didn't begin to compare with the physical pregnancy.

I went into maternity clothes at six weeks. The body that used to stand at attention like the Marine in a recruitment poster looked like a soufflé after someone had just slammed the oven door. Any skin that didn't sag was swollen. The parts of the body were never in the same place two days in a row. When I sucked in my stomach nothing moved. I had morning sickness, swollen feet, leg cramps, heartburn, and chair paralysis. (The latter is the inability to get out of a chair once you are in it.) My hair would not curl and my bladder shrank to the size of a lentil.

My husband said I was the most beautiful woman he had ever seen. Great! I would not only have two children under the age of two in a house the size of a phone booth, I now had a husband with training wheels on his brain.

Despite all of that, it was a wonderful time of our lives. We loved babies and felt blessed to have them. Besides, after a woman has given birth, she attains nirvana. For twenty-four hours (or thirty days depending on how long you can, excuse the expression, milk it) you are a living shrine.

You have given the ultimate gift to your husband, who before now has taken back everything else you've ever given him and credited it to the account. You have fulfilled your mother's wildest dreams of revenge. You have given your father a picture for his billfold to replace Ann Miller. You have

enough stretch marks to spread guilt for two
fur coats, a quartz watch, and a trip to St.
Croix in January. Presenting your husband
with a baby is the quintessential headache.

We named the baby Andrew and brought
him home down a street lined with people
hoisting palms and honking horns. Five cars
in the driveway belonging to grandparents
and friends awaited his arrival. As he slept in
the small basket in our bedroom, three people
watched him breathe and the rest hovered
around me like I was a rock star.

Casseroles appeared like miracles from
nowhere. Friends chirped, "Let's get together
soon." Grandparents begged to "sit" if we
wanted to get out.

We never saw those people again.

Our marriage settled down to routine and
predictability. The maintenance of two children was awesome. Their teeth didn't come
in right. Their feet toed inward. They were
allergic to cheap food. If they didn't get a
Slinky toy that appeared on TV, their heart
rate would become faint. They were like
appliances. They only broke down on weekends, when the prices went up.

We adored them, but the reality was they
were the boat that we were going to dock at a
marina on Lake Erie . . . the trip to the

How Much Happiness Can We Finance?

Bahamas we were going to take when we got a few bucks ahead . . . the little two-seater sports car that would take ten years off our lives . . . the model home with two bathrooms we lusted after.

When Andrew was three years old, I discovered I was pregnant again. My friends said, "Get it over with before you get your shape back and the red rash leaves your hands."

The problem of an uneven number in the family did not escape me. There were only four chairs that came with our dinette. Where would it sit? There were four Twinkies to a package. Who does without? There were only two car windows in the back seat of the car. I would never know peace again.

Not only that, the kids were in the majority. The vote would always stand: adults, 2; children, 3. We would be outvoted on the puppy who was trained to chair legs, which movies to see, which TV shows to watch, and where we would spend our vacations. As parents, we were in a no-win situation. We had lost control and were a minority in our own family.

The trip home from the hospital with Matthew was different. A surly sitter wanted combat pay for staying with the other two. They had been living on a diet of popcorn and cola. The dog was pregnant and chased cars. The older child bit, the middle one spit, and my mother said I had better start to sit on them or they would be taken over by the state. I had just given birth to a seven-pound twelve-ounce baby and was four pounds heavier than when I delivered.

Nothing in our married lives would ever make such an impact as the arrival of children. The five of us would share the same diseases, relatives, and toothpaste. We would rarely agree on anything. We would slam doors in one another's faces, tell lies to get what we wanted, comfort one another, hide food, charge interest for money loaned. We would chew one another's gum. All of us would spend the rest of our lives trying to please one another.

The privacy that a married couple enjoys B.C. (Before Children) no longer exists. There are no OFF LIMITS, DO NOT ENTER, or PERSONNEL ONLY signs that are obeyed. There is a revolving door on your lives that invites kids in during sex, showers, telephone conversations, naps, or vacations. Children had changed our entire lives. I was no longer "Erma." I was somebody's mother. I would have been someone's wife had I not been ironing or packing lunches at 11 P.M.

With stay-at-home moms, 90 percent of

the child-raising was left to them. The role of fathers at home was a bit part . . . a walk-on. He took all the pictures because he knew how to load and unload the camera. He was not afraid to go into the basement by himself. He tightened up the clothesline so it wouldn't sag. As for child-raising, he came in every evening and tossed them up to the ceiling until they threw up from laughter.

I hid my dreams in the back of my mind— it was the only safe place in the house. From time to time I would get them out and play with them, not daring to reveal them to anyone else because they were fragile and might get broken.

I wanted to return to writing, but what if I tried and failed? Then I would have nothing left to hang on to.

Maybe all I could do was mother. I removed spots, scrubbed toilets, killed roaches, polished shoes, cleaned ears, planted trees, blew up balloons, hustled food, kept laundry moving, counseled, disciplined, listened, mediated disputes, answered phones, transmitted messages, volunteered, cut toenails, and enforced house rules. I knew all the words to the Mouseketeers' theme song. Some résumé.

And yet, why did I feel so fulfilled when I

bedded down three kids between clean sheets? What if raising and instilling values in three children and turning them into worthwhile human beings would be the most important contribution I ever made in my lifetime? And if this were true . . . then how come someone didn't tell me?

Bill and I weren't unique. From 1949 to 1965, our generation gave birth to 77 million children whose impressive numbers would earn them the label of "baby boomers." Parenting was an epidemic that was to have an impact on every phase of our society from schools, health care, marketing, banks, morals, and the building industry. Especially the building industry.

We had waited so long for children, we felt we were on a roll. Our lives had never been so enriched. Bill suggested we go for the twelve apostles. After all, we already had Andrew and Matthew behind us.

I looked around the four-room house that had children stacked like cords of wood. If I gave birth to John, Philip, Bartholomew, Thomas, Thaddaeus, Judas, two Simons, and a pair of Jameses, I'd have to hang them from the ceiling on meat hooks. (I'd also be in an institution braiding my hair.)

"We need more space," I said. "I think it's

time we cashed in the nest egg you've been sitting on since the army."

"It's not enough," said Bill.

"Then we'll have to borrow."

"I refuse to borrow from our parents again," he said emphatically. "We walk into their homes and we're six years old."

"Then what's the alternative?" I asked. "Rob a bank?"

"We're too clumsy. You could sell your body on the street."

"Forget it, I'm too tired," I said.

"Your parents have offered to help."

"I know," I said, "but we'd get the save-the-pennies-in-the-mason-jar-and-they'll-grow speech."

"It's either that or my parents will tell us how they never saw a movie until they were thirty-five."

We pulled into my parents' driveway in a car they had when it was new. We must have sat there for five minutes without speaking. I was looking at their large house with the rolling lawn and the porch furniture protected with plastic. Inside were two bathrooms with lids down on the toilets, two bedrooms that were never used, a fireplace where wood never burned, and living room sofas that had never been sat on.

Erma Bombeck

It wasn't fair. I wanted steaks while I could still chew them. I wanted to go out to dinner while I still knew where I was. My mom and dad hung around the beaches of Hawaii while I spent the best years of my life waiting for the washer repairman.

I took a deep breath and we rang the doorbell.

As we awkwardly sat down at their kitchen table, my mother poured me a half glass of milk and cautioned, "Don't spill it." Bill took the plunge. "We need to borrow $1,500 for a bigger house." It was a bitter moment for us. We weren't two mature parents. We were just two kids playing grown-up. We still needed Mommy and Daddy's permission, blessings, and money to survive.

For Richer or for Poorer

❧

I was watching the old Bob Newhart Show *one* night when Bob slipped into his check-balancing costume . . . a baggy sweater over a sports shirt, topped off with half glasses perched on the end of his nose.

Poor Emily. She didn't realize it, but we were married to the same man. Every time Bill cleared off the dining room table and appeared in an old sweater with patches on the sleeves, I felt like the Bonanno family up for audit.

As he shuffled through the canceled checks and put an X next to the entry in the checkbook, he would pause from time to time and ask me a question.

Erma Bombeck

"You have D.M. penciled in this entry. What does that mean?"

"It means 'didn't mail' so you add it to the balance instead of subtract."

"I see . . . and 'S.M.'?"

"Are you sure I wrote that?"

"It's written in blue eyeliner," he said dryly.

"It stands for See Me. I must have recorded that check somewhere. Give me a minute." I dumped the contents of my handbag out on the table and a white breath mint rolled out on the table. "Here it is . . . check number 936 for $10.85."

"Let me have it."

"Or maybe it's check number 1085 for $9.36."

At our house I was the keeper of the checkbook. Don't ask me why. For every woman like me who complained about having to pay all the bills, there were ten women married to men who doled out money as if giving an allowance to a ten-year-old who had just finished cutting the grass.

Some women even had squirrel funds where they hid their mad money in empty Alka-Seltzer boxes behind the heating pads in the back of linen closets and dreamed of running away from home.

For Richer or for Poorer

In our marriage, it didn't matter if we were a one or a two paycheck family. We just deposited everything we had and I spent it. It worked for me.

What didn't work for me was spending money with my husband. If I shopped with him we couldn't sleep in the same bed that night without opening a window to let out all the hostility.

The problem seemed to lie in our motivation for shopping. I bought in haste and repented in leisure. He shopped like he was gathering data for a doctoral dissertation.

As Bill pored over the checkbook, he paused from time to time to take off his glasses and rub his eyes. Then he put them on and once again punched up a new bunch of figures on the calculator. "This notation here," he said, sliding the checkbook under my nose, "did you write OK?"

"Yes."

"I take that to mean a verification of a check you have written and recorded and have the money in the bank to cover?"

"It stands for 'Only Kidding.' I just put down a deposit to hold some drapery fabric until I thought about it. You don't really think I'd spend $35 a yard for drapery material, do you?"

"So I . . . "

"Add it," I ordered.

Usually by the end of the evening I could see the handwriting on the wall. The checkbook did not balance, would not balance in our lifetime, and the account would have to be closed. He would turn to me and announce, "You must find a new bank again."

I always had a good feeling when he said that. It was like God giving me a second chance. There is always something spiritual and cleansing about walking into a new bank where they don't know you and having them smile and say, "How may I help you?"

There's an innocence to embarking on a new checking account. It must have been the way Adam and Eve felt when they were standing naked in the Garden of Eden . . . full of wonderment and anticipation.

I am always hopeful that the new bank will have personnel with a sense of humor. I want to believe their little commercials that show a banker with a merry twinkle in his eye whom I can poke with my elbow and say, "Can't you take a joke? Where would I get $5,000?"

I want to feel they are sensitive to all those little human frailties like 7s that look like 2s and the checks on which I filled in the

"For" line with, "the love of God, don't cash until after the 15th."

A new bank was titillating, but it didn't begin to compare with the first credit card with my name on it. I understood the principle behind check writing. For every dollar you wrote on a check, in theory you should have a dollar in the bank to cover it.

I never got a handle on the credit card. I just knew it was magic and I never left home without it.

A lot of marriages don't survive credit cards. Patience is no longer a virtue and if you want it now, it is yours . . . with Godfather interest.

After a few unchecked buying sprees where I amassed a debt larger than the national budget of Brazil, Tokyo, and Australia combined, Bill climbed into his check-balancing costume one night and summoned me to the dining room table. "Have you seen San Quentin?" he asked.

"Only in pictures."

"It is going to be your home if you don't stop writing checks and charging. Where's the checkbook?"

"I lost it again. Maybe I could open an account in a new bank."

"There are no more new banks. We would

have to move to a new city to find a new bank. We'll just have to go to the old one and tell them what happened."

"No," I said, "I do not deserve another chance. I am not good with money and I am even worse with bookkeeping. I wouldn't blame you if you took away the checkbook and every time I want a blank check I would have to come to you."

"Are you sure this is what you want?" he asked.

"Positive."

A few weeks later, I found the checkbook on the back of the commode under a copy of *Good Housekeeping*. I was ecstatic. When I told Bill about it he said, "That account is no longer working. I closed it out."

"What do you mean you closed it out?" I asked.

"You told me to," he said.

If that isn't a crock! Married to a man for all these years and you think he knows you. I guess I should have put OK (Only Kidding!) in the margin of his new checkbook.

1959

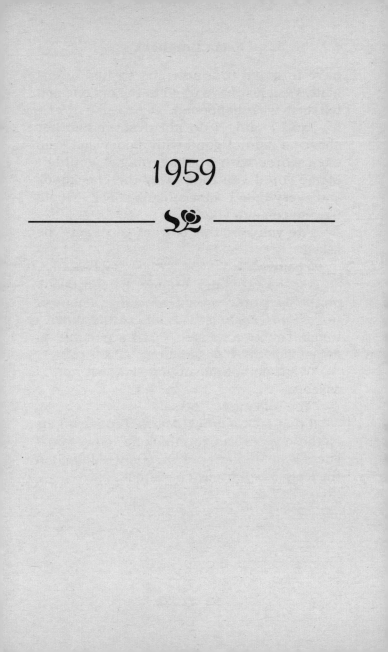

Reunion

It was a room that was too big for the event.

All the balloons and all the streamers in the world wouldn't have given it intimacy. Small tables and chairs hugged the walls like security blankets. At one end was the proverbial table holding a punch bowl and snacks. At the other was a five-piece band sawing away under a banner that read WELCOME CLASS OF 1949.

Bill and I paused at the door to take it all in. "Make a note," I said, "if it looks like a lot of people aren't going to show up for my funeral, hold it in a phone booth so it'll look crowded."

Erma Bombeck

"Who are these people?" he asked.

I shook my head.

"I should have crammed the yearbook," he mused. "You know how bad I am at remembering names."

"I got a trick that always works," I said. "Just say, 'Erma, I want you to meet . . . ' then pause just long enough for the woman to say, 'Cindy . . . Cindy Johnson' and then you say, 'I know that. I just couldn't remember your married name.' Works every time."

A member of the committee slapped a name tag over my left bosom. "What shall we name the other one?" I smiled. She was not amused.

Coming here was a big mistake. Reunions are like report cards in your life that come out every ten years to tally up how you're progressing. They're like a horse race where you all start off together at the sound of the bell and you have this self-punishing desire to know who finishes first.

An unfamiliar person positioned her body in front of Bill with a grin on her face. He smiled back and said, "Erma, I want you to meet . . . " (He paused on cue.)

"Sister Mary Elizabeth," said the classmate.

Bill said, "I know that. I just couldn't remember why you never married."

Reunion

Who came to these things anyway?

Insurance salesmen who light up a room by leaving it. They figure one class reunion is worth 500 callbacks.

Old cheerleaders always return. Especially the ones whose bust measurements exceed their IQs by 35.

People who know all the words to the school song always show up. Both of them.

I don't know what I expected after ten years.

We were a boring class. We were the ones the teachers talked about in their private lounge and begged forgiveness for inflicting us on society.

We didn't protest anything . . . not war, not foreign policies, not even the fact that there were fifteen parking spaces on campus for 1,500 students.

We were basically a bunch of losers. We scheduled a pep assembly on Good Friday. We elected a class president who dropped out of school. As our class gift, we left the school a drinking fountain that rusted. We were so square our phys ed teacher got bombed and eloped with our guidance counselor on prom night and we brought them back.

Our graduates had been as predictable as

their class prophecies. The class clown went into local politics, and the girl most likely to . . . did.

We were a generation born too late to eat goldfish and too early to flash.

Throughout the night there was an uncomfortable feeling that our contemporaries were going to find out more about us than we were willing for them to know.

Did they suspect we had to leave at the stroke of twelve because the baby-sitter charged seventy-five cents an hour after midnight?

Did they know I was a terrible mother who put off taking her child to a doctor for an ear infection until after the fifteenth of the month because we didn't get paid until the fifteenth?

Did they have a clue that if I wasn't wearing a girdle to compress my body, I would bump into opposite walls at the same time?

Did they know that Bill, who had a Masters in education, delivered mail during the Christmas holidays?

Most of my classmates were married and with the slightest twitch of interest would whip out a folder of baby pictures that dropped to the floor like a yo-yo.

They had beat the national average.

Reunion

Experts predicted the average marriage ends in divorce at six and a half years. That's when the happiness warranty suddenly expires. It wasn't too hard to figure out why.

At the end of seventy-eight months, a bride will have cooked 5,408 meals. It's as good or as bad as it's going to get.

You will have met all the relatives—away from the church—and know which ones never to lend money to.

The pretenses go. Company manners are put aside. Courtesies are no longer a consideration. His feet have started to smell. She leaves toothpaste globs in the sink. He cleans his fingernails at the table. She doesn't just blow her nose. She flushes it.

At seventy-eight months, the trousseau is faded and ragged. The see-through nightgown is worn with underwear and wool socks. The wedding proofs have faded on command from the photographer, who doesn't want you to get anything for nothing.

There are usually children to occupy every minute of your waking hours and some of your sleeping ones.

Affection has all the passion of giving mouth-to-mouth resuscitation to a dead parakeet.

There was something sad about "settling

in." How I was always awed by the class slut, Janice. She used to slip out after lunch and meet one of the teachers in the cemetery behind the university. Someone said she had on a sun-back dress one day and, if she stood with her back to a mirror, one could read, OUR BELOVED MOTHER 1853–1926, but I think it just made a good story.

Janice, who had given new meaning to the words, "Made in America," married and brought her accountant husband to the reunion.

We had all done what was expected of us.

There was a drumroll and the class secretary asked for our attention. Darlene won the award for having the most children. She was the mother of six and won a croquet set. (Great gift for a woman who hadn't seen her feet in ten years—let alone a wicket.)

Ted, who lived in Chicago, won a pen and pencil set for traveling the greatest distance to attend the reunion, and my idol, Janice, was awarded a dinner for two at Ruby's Steak House for being the alumna no one recognized. (Probably because she was upright.)

It was fun visiting the past for a few hours. We remembered those years as good ones, when we had no responsibility and nothing in our future but promises.

Reunion

We all lied to one another with our screams of "You haven't changed a bit!" But we knew better. It was more than women growing a little thicker around the middle and the men combing their hair in creative patterns to cover barren spots. We had changed. The couple who went to a drive-in and who you couldn't see daylight between now sat at opposite sides of the table. He talked about how he rotated his tires last weekend and she exchanged a tuna casserole recipe with her friend.

In the background, the band was playing "Stardust." It would be another ten years before Peggy Lee would put our fears to lyrics, "Is That All There Is?"

What Are Friends For?

❧❧

Every day thousands of cars snaked out of the cities in an unending line to make their pilgrimage to "Our Lady of Suburbia." It was a shrine of giant proportions where wives and their 2.4 children kept vigil.

Men visited these temples each evening and on weekends. It gave them sustenance for their hard work and reinforced their quest for success.

But the women who feasted at this spiritual table every day were bored out of their skulls. That is why they clung to friends, who were life rafts bobbing in a sea of high fevers,

What Are Friends For?

dead batteries, strained lamb, unmade beds, and unpaid bills.

We saw one another more than we saw our husbands or our children. We shared our innermost secrets . . . things we never told the man we married because we were sure he wouldn't understand.

We also commiserated among ourselves as to what we had gotten ourselves into. Without these friendships, one of us would surely have made headlines for doing something violent.

I lived in a house between Helen and Charmaine. We had the same floor plan. All together, we had nine children, two college degrees, eight car pools, and three husbands who thought all we did all day was drink coffee and push buttons.

In our daily therapy sessions, we discovered that men change after marriage. When we were joined in holy wedlock, they were social animals. The day after the honeymoon, they changed into bedroom slippers and a coat-sweater and their heartbeats dropped to levels somewhere between comatose and death.

At our house, going out for an evening was like playing "Twenty Questions":

"Who's going to be at this party?"

Erma Bombeck

"Will there be a place to sit down and talk or do I have to stand around eating bait off of crackers for three hours?"

"What time are we coming home?"

"Am I going to have a good time?"

There was no doubt about it. I married adventure.

There was a time when we used to dance. I thought he enjoyed holding me in his arms and talking into my hair. Now I am hearing, "It's too crowded. Wait till the crowd thins out."

"'Moon River' is too fast. Let's wait till the tempo slows down a bit."

"The song is almost finished. Let's wait until next New Year's."

"We just got here an hour ago. Give me a chance to talk."

"Why didn't you mention you wanted to dance before I unbuttoned my jacket?"

The three suburbanites hungered for conversation of the outside world and appreciation for what we did. There was only one woman in the entire plat who left the house each day to go into the city. Her name was Betty and she had no children. We used to gather at our picture windows and watch her tool by in her sports car. We had no idea where she went or what she did when she got there. When someone was new to the neighborhood, we would point out Betty's house and why it was special. It looked like ours but it was different. Betty and her husband didn't have muddy holes around the garbage cans made by kids who cut across the lawn too many times. They had little stepping stones. Their snow never had ruts from sled runners or snowmen with one eye. It was always pristine like a Christmas card. Betty always had a theme arrangement by her doorbell . . . mistletoe for Christmas, corn husks for Halloween, ribbons for Easter. All we ever had were OUT OF ORDER signs.

In our hearts, we knew she and her husband bathed together in a bathtub lit by candles and sipped champagne. None of our husbands talked anymore. Mine was like a hostile witness.

"What do you want for dinner?" I'd ask Bill.

"I don't care."

"We're having liver."

"I hate liver."

"I thought you didn't care. Maybe if you talked more I'd know what you like."

"What do you want me to say?"

"Do you love me?"

"What a question."

"Say it!"

"OK, I love you."

"Don't say it like you're ordering lunch."

"I love you."

"I don't believe you."

Sometimes, it seemed like all of us were married to the same man. All started their vacations at four in the morning. (That's an oxymoron if ever I heard one.)

They refused to admit they were lost and would never ask directions anywhere.

Someone very wise once observed that marriages fail because husbands and wives see one another at the worst possible times of the day. They don't get the best of one another.

There is a lot to that. Mornings were not good for either one of us. During the night, everything had wrinkled . . . our skins, the clothes to be worn that day, the lunch meat. In the evening, we were in a hurry to get to the end of another day. Somehow husbands never gave their wives the praise they gave the secretary who moistened the sponge on their desk for stamps.

Wives didn't have the same tingle of excitement when their husbands pulled into the driveway as they did when their parking tickets were validated in the dentist's office.

What Are Friends For?

With Helen and Charmaine I could share it all. There was a comfortableness and an understanding that wasn't there with my spouse. I wondered if men had such an outlet for their feelings. Did they dump on their male friends, or did they just sit around a card table all night and say, "I call. What have you got?"

Bill kept in touch with all his old friends, but if they confided in one another and shared the intimacies of their lives he never talked about it.

One Sunday, we were visiting Ed (our best man) and his wife for a backyard barbecue. Ed announced he was going to have open heart surgery the next week. He was pretty cavalier about it, so we were too. We'd get together when he was up and about.

Ed never came home.

Hours after his surgery he died at the age of thirty-three.

Bill went off by himself. I stood at the door and didn't know what to say. We must have realized at that moment that neither of us had ever handled pain of such magnitude. We didn't know what to do. Our parents had always done the mourning for us. We had always looked to them for assurance that things were going to be all right. If something hurt, they just made it better with anything from a kiss on the knee to the promise of ice cream. They had made death seem so simple with their pat phrases of, "She lived a good, long life," or "He was just plain worn out." What did we tell ourselves about Ed? He hadn't lived a long life and he wasn't worn out. He was thirty-three years old!

Our contemporaries weren't supposed to die. Our grandparents? Of course. Our parents? Possibly. But not our generation. We were faced not only with the loss of one of our own, but with our own mortality.

My God! We were not going to live forever. Youth didn't carry a guarantee. Wouldn't you have thought someone would have warned us? What had we done with our lives so far to justify our years? Were we really living it or were we just existing from day to day? What was really important? Ring around the collar? Or spending time with your husband? Would anyone notice I had eradicated yellow wax build up in my kitchen, or would my children remember me as a mother who never had time to listen to their stories at the end of the day?

When I heard the news, my reaction was instinctive. I gathered my friends around me. Not Bill, but my friends. With them, feelings came out easily. They were shocked and compassionate and said all the right things, but somehow I was not comforted. I needed intimacy and warmth.

The house was quiet. As I passed the doorway to our bedroom I could see the silhouette of my husband sitting on the bed, his shoulders slumped and his head bowed. He looked so alone and I wanted to carry some of the hurt, but I didn't know how.

Here was a man with whom I had shared three children, a home, and a life for twelve years and yet we didn't know one another well enough to cry together.

Our marriage had never taken either of us to this level before. It had always been like a business with each of us carrying out our individual roles. He was the provider and I was the nurturer who could handle anything. Not to handle "it," whatever it was, was perceived as a weakness.

I was going to reach out and touch his shoulder, but instead started to walk away. Then his voice broke the silence. "We used to play in the dirt together in the alley behind the garage," he said quietly.

I made a place for myself beside him on the edge of the bed. "He arranged our first date with one another," I added.

Erma Bombeck

Slowly, awkwardly, with tears streaming down our faces, we reluctantly reached out to one another. Neither of us knew how much strength we had to give, but we were willing to share it. We gave one another something that most friendships are not able to give—vulnerability. Throughout our years together, we had built up a history and a closeness so subtle even we didn't know it was there. On that evening, we admitted we couldn't handle life alone. We needed one another.

On that evening, for the second time Ed had brought us together. Had Bill not been there for me or I for him, this probably would have been a shorter book.

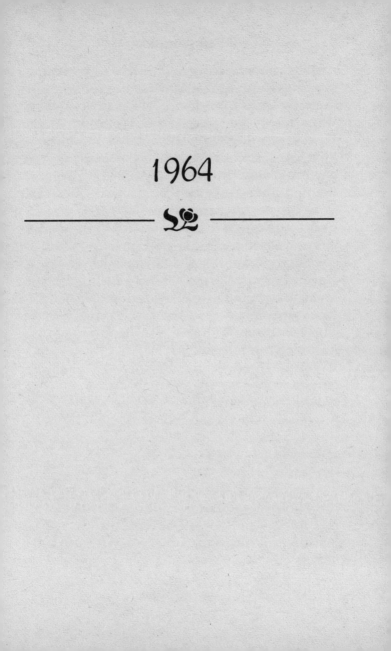

1964

Empty Nest

———————— ❧ ————————

We turned up our jacket collars to ward off the September morning chill as we huddled together near the bus stop. One young mother fumbled nervously in her pocket for a cigarette. The air was charged with anticipation and tension. No one spoke.

A few feet from us was a group of six year olds wearing clothes with the cardboard and pins freshly removed, clutching shiny lunch boxes and looking like they were going to be sick.

It was a scene right out of a World War II movie of American troops just before they hit the beaches of Normandy.

Erma Bombeck

My eyes rested on my youngest—a small, red-haired child I had parked at the curb. He clutched a small note in his hand with four letters on it, B-O-Y-S, with instructions, "Match it up to a door and you get to pee."

What could be going through his mind at this moment? What indeed . . .

My name is Matt and I don't know anything.

What if the school bus jerks after I get on and I lose my balance and my pants rip and everyone laughs?

What if the wind blows all the important papers out of my hands that I'm supposed to take home?

What if I spend a whole day without a friend?

The large yellow bus groaned as it turned the corner and loomed like a behemoth. It ground to a stop and swallowed up the small group of children before our eyes.

As it jerked into first gear and disappeared from our view, a mighty cheer went up from the women. "Mother's Day is over!" shouted one. "I'll drink to that!" yelled another. "I feel like I've just been on a diet and lost fifty-seven pounds," giggled her friend. We all made promises to get together and celebrate by eating something decadent.

We all went home and cried.

Empty Nest

At dinner that night, Bill acted like it was just another day. I think he said, "How did it go?"

"How did it go?" I had just lost the longest job I ever held. At thirty-seven I was too old for an income from the Tooth Fairy and too young for Social Security. I had no idea what I was going to do with the rest of my life, and he wanted to know, "How did it go?"

It never occurred to him what could be going through my mind at this moment. What indeed . . .

My name is Erma and I don't know anything. How do I keep busy for the next forty years?

What if I apply for a real job and the only references I have are three kids who swear I lock them outside to play when the chill factor is 20 degrees below?

What if I go back to school and have to bring a note from my mother excusing my hot flashes?

What if I enter the Miss Pillsbury Bake-Off and only win Miss Congeniality?

What if all my friends get jobs outside of their homes and I get stuck with all their kids who throw up and have to be picked up at school before the end of the day?

What if my husband outgrows me mentally

and starts to shop for someone who has read something more current than a steam iron warranty?

How long will it be before I vacuum the carpet right into the concrete flooring?

It was the end—or the beginning—of an era for both my son and me, depending on how you looked at it.

If my husband cared or understood, it was not apparent. He had a job that he was immersed in. Teaching school was fulfilling, challenging, and occupied all of his days and some of his evenings.

Actually, he fitted the workaholic profile to a T. I compared him to the actor Laurence Harvey. He told the story of how at one time he threatened to commit suicide by putting his head in a gas oven.

When his head was in there, however, he discovered the oven was thick with grease and he decided to clean it. "By the time the bloody thing was clean, I'd gone off the whole idea," he later said.

That was Bill. When we went on a picnic, he sat at the table and balanced the checkbook. If he was in the bathroom, he'd read something . . . anything . . . even if it was the American Journal on Tooth Decay.

Every time he was near a phone, he

reached out absently and untangled the cord. While he was waiting for a traffic light, he busied himself cleaning out the glove compartment.

My mother's solution to life's problems was, "Take a laxative." His advice was, "Relax and enjoy it."

That was his answer to my empty nest crisis.

One night as we readied for bed I said, "I have to find something to do. I not only visited my meat in the frozen food locker today, I had a good time."

"I don't get it," he said, scratching his stomach. "You've worked hard all these years raising kids and cleaning the house. Now is the time to sit back and enjoy the fruits of your labor. You've earned it. You don't have to work. We've got enough to get by and maybe even take a vacation. Besides, do you want to end up like Bonnie?"

Bonnie lived two blocks over from us. She was the dark side of Donna Reed. Never brought the groceries in from the car unless they were perishable. She took them out of the grocery bags as she needed them. The family never used real plates or silverware. The bread and the lunch meat were served at the table right out of their wrappers. She ironed only on demand.

Erma Bombeck

One day, Bonnie said she had had it. She hired a cleaning woman to come in and sit with her children while she went out to work. She got a job in a day nursery where her cleaning woman left her kids off in the morning. The irony escaped no one.

I understood Bonnie. We lived in a society where you were paid what you were worth. Being a wife and mother provided lodgings, clothing, food allowance, a minimum dental plan, and a few health benefits. It certainly made no provisions for forced or early retirement.

I envied Bonnie. At least she filled up her days.

Most of us in the neighborhood were in this period of restlessness when Charmaine called one October day in 1964 and said she had tickets to attend a lecture in the Town Hall series by Betty Friedan, author of a recently published book, *The Feminine Mystique*.

None of us had heard of Betty Friedan, but we would have watched a slide show on the History of Paper Clips to get out of the daily drudge detail. We all climbed in Charmaine's station wagon with the wood on it and set off to be entertained.

Winds of Revolution

The small, stocky, mussed woman took her place on the barren stage. We were cheered. She looked like one of us. Then she began to describe our lives: screaming children, dirty laundry, and grandmothers who refused to sit. We were giddy with anticipation. She was going to put it all in perspective for us and make us laugh.

Instead, she admonished us from the stage, throwing us into a dead silence. "This is not funny!" she charged. "I am talking about a disease with no name. This is a battle to emancipate women!" We all felt like we were back in grade school and had just been caught chewing gum before we could swallow it.

Erma Bombeck

For the next hour, she was on the attack, the target being our lives. "You must not only question, 'Who am I?' You must dare to answer the question."

She told us to eradicate forever the words, "just a housewife." "Marriage and motherhood are essential parts of life—but not the whole of it."

She cautioned us to experience personal growth to keep up with our husbands. She said women don't need men to feel alive, nor do they need to live through their husbands and children.

"This is a sexist society," she shouted. "You are not using your God-given abilities to their potential."

There was some truth to what she was saying, but there was an uneasiness in the audience that had been ordered how to react. We were too intimidated to laugh and too old to cry. We sat there stunned.

She had dared to suggest that the role for which our mothers had groomed us—taking care of a husband and family—was wrong. We should think of ourselves first.

That morning Betty Friedan had counted on an anger among women in her Midwestern audience that did not yet exist.

We didn't realize it, but in those few

hours we had all been impregnated with the seeds of a movement of monumental proportions . . . one that would grow inside us and affect us all of our lives whether we embraced it or not. Not one woman throughout the world would escape being touched or affected by it in some way. Our relationships and attitudes toward marriage, children, and family would never be the same again.

When the speaker left the stage, the three of us sat quietly without speaking. We were the women Betty Friedan needed to reach . . . educated, thinking women who were starved for challenges. Finally, Helen spoke. "Let's have lunch at King Cole's. They validate." A cheer went up.

We couldn't get Betty Friedan's remarks out of our minds. At lunch we questioned why we were the only ones in the house capable of changing a toilet tissue spindle. We wondered why when a child laughed, he belonged to Daddy, and when he had a sagging diaper that smelled like a landfill—"He wants his mother."

When we painted the living room, how come men got the big rollers and slapped paint on the walls and we always got the lousy woodwork and windowpanes?

Betty was right. Homemakers had no

heroines . . . no champions . . . no leadership . . . no unions . . . and no one who knew what we did, let alone appreciated it.

And yet, what were we supposed to do? Walk out? It wasn't that simple.

I bought a copy of *The Feminine Mystique* and read every word of it. I found myself defending my life. Maybe because I felt threatened and frightened by the changes she proposed.

Also, she had come down hard on three of my favorite writers—Jean Kerr, Phyllis McGinley, and Shirley Jackson—housewives who, according to her words, "reveled in a comic world of children's pranks and eccentric washing machines and parents' night at the PTA."

Ms. Friedan observed there is something about housewife writers that isn't funny—like Uncle Tom or Amos and Andy. She said just telling bored, trapped, desperate, empty women that "we're all in this mess together" is not a joke.

Well, maybe Ms. Friedan couldn't laugh in a world of washing machines that devoured socks and coat hangers that enjoyed an active sex life, but I had to. I needed humor desperately. I had a life going here. Maybe it needed work, but I had a husband and three kids whom I loved and I wasn't ready to discard anything until I was sure what was going to replace it. But I liked the part about using your God-given potential. I wondered if I had any.

A few weeks later, I walked into a suburban weekly newspaper and asked for a job as a housewife-columnist who "reveled in a comic world of children's pranks, eccentric washing machines, and parents' night at the PTA."

Later, when my husband came home, I said, "Guess what? I got a part-time job today."

"Doing what?" he asked.

"I'm going to write about funny things that happen to our family."

"You can't be serious," he said. "You're going to expose our personal lives to the public, exploit our children, and hold up our intimate moments together for the world to see?"

"I get three bucks a column," I said.

He smiled. "Why didn't you say so?"

What happened to me during the next year was like a chapter right out of a Danielle Steel novel. An editor, Glenn Thompson, spotted my $3-a-week column on domesticity in the neighborhood weekly and asked me to write for his daily. Within three weeks, he brought it to the attention of a Long Island newspaper syndicate that agreed to distribute it nationally if I could write three a week.

That night in bed, I couldn't get to sleep. This was a major decision that could affect our marriage big time. I had promised to love, honor, and obey (with windows and floors thrown in). Now, I was changing the rules. I wanted to write, travel, and trade quips with Johnny Carson. How would this affect my children? Would my husband look at me as a competitor? Would my writing career expand and eventually outgrow my other one as a wife and mother? What if there were distractions and cleaning toilet bowls wouldn't be fun anymore? Would extra burdens be put on my family because of my selfish desire to reach out for something challenging?

I announced the next morning that I had an offer that might possibly make me a household word—like mildew or bleach. My daughter was the only one who reacted to it. She said, "I hope you can still drive me to Scouts on Tuesdays."

By all odds, this should be the most important chapter in this book on marriage.

Winds of Revolution

Weaving a career into the fabric of a traditional family should have thrown five lives into upheaval. Priorities should have been shuffled. Responsibilities reassigned. Relationships threatened.

It didn't cause so much as a ripple.

No one noticed the dynamo that raced through the house faster than aspirin racing to the bloodstream . . . more powerful than a detergent with built-in bleach and able to leap over three kids to get dinner to the table. They walked around the ironing board that was set up in the living room at night without so much as a "Why are you ironing at midnight?" They didn't have a clue that the mild-mannered woman who snapped beans and sewed in name tags at night, by day wrote speeches, made deadlines, and was SUPERMOM!

I wasn't the only woman running on empty. One of my friends called one morning to tell me she was worried about herself. On the night she conceived her third daughter, she was mentally planning a brunch for ten people and removing old nail polish. "Am I a Supermom?" she asked. During the next few years, I became a cottage industry. Bill got a wooden door from the lumberyard and balanced it over two stacks of cement blocks in our bedroom for a desk. From there I wrote books and columns, speeches, and answered the trickle of fan mail.

I also starched collars, laundered shoe-strings, beat carpets, and vacuumed the bed-springs every April. I baked cakes from scratch, hosed out my garbage cans every week with bleach, and saved antifreeze from my car to save a few bucks. No one ever saw me with my blinds down or my toilet seat up.

But the cry for help from mothers who worked outside the home was becoming louder and louder. Stories began to appear that men should shoulder some of the domestic chores as well as share some of the burden of child raising.

Late one night in the kitchen as I was slapping mustard on a chorus line of white bread for the next day's lunches, I felt a presence at my elbow.

"Aren't you about finished?" he asked.

"I got another hour out here."

There was a pause before he put his hands on my shoulders and turned me toward him. "For months," he said, "I've watched you kill yourself trying to work and keep all of this going. I think it's time I pitched in. From here on in, I'm going to make the coffee every morning."

You'd have thought he just said, "Let me carry the baby during the last three months."

I don't mean to sound ungrateful, but throwing a few beans in a pot of water is to women on the same domestic entry level as putting the spring back in the toilet tissue holder. It's nice, but it certainly doesn't compare with swishing your hand around a toilet bowl rim or taking lint off corduroy pants that were washed with a nose tissue in the pocket.

But for a man in the '60s it was like compromising his masculinity. "That's nice," I said. "Now do you suppose that one day you might open up a cupboard door and put a box of cereal on the table?"

He stiffened. "You're becoming strident," he said, "and it's unattractive."

"I'm not being strident," I said, "just practical. There's no reason why you sit in the living room every night and wait to be summoned to the kitchen like you're being invited to a cotillion. This is an Equal Opportunity establishment. Everyone is welcome to pitch in."

The next night I was poised over a stack of frozen hamburger patties. I was trying to separate them by balancing a large meat cleaver between the slices and tapping the handle with a rolling pin. A voice at my elbow said, "You are going to cut your hand off when that knife slips."

"Are there no surprises in life?" I sighed.

"I'm just trying to help," Bill said. "I've noticed that you also poke lettuce down a spinning disposer. You keep doing that and you'll never play Frisbee with your right hand as long as you live."

"Are you finished?"

"No. Why don't you get yourself some pot holders? Every time you take a hot casserole out of the oven balanced between two forks, I cringe. Also, someone should clean that toaster and line it with foil. The fires are getting too big for you to smother with a loaf of French bread."

"I know what I'm doing," I said testily.

"And these spices. If I ran an office the way you run this kitchen, I'd never find anything. I'm going to put them in some kind of order."

"Don't do that."

"Your dishes are all wrong. The ones you use the most should be on the bottom shelf where you can get to them."

"Please."

"Your manuals for your appliances are all over the place. I'm going to put them all in one notebook. What in the world is this?"

"It's a cookie sheet."

"It looks like the cardboard I put under my car to catch oil drippings. How much do these things cost?"

"I don't know . . . ninety-nine cents . . . a dollar forty-nine."

"We're a two-income family now and we can't afford a new cookie sheet?"

"Get out of my kitchen!"

"I thought you wanted help."

"Not that bad."

Actually, he was proud of my career. Most of the guilt I felt was self-inflicted. As long as I was fussy about my kids' peanut butter, I could say yes to a commencement speech on Mother's Day. If I made a tuna noodle casserole and left a note to my daughter to slide it in a 350-degree oven and brought her a present when I came home in time for dinner, I could do *The Mike Douglas Show*. As long as my husband smelled his bath towel and looked like he had just seen God, I felt I was allowed to pursue a career for another week. To complain would have left me open for, "No one asked you to work. You can quit any time."

All the wages from both our paychecks went into one account and we shared. All the daily experiences of our individual jobs were exchanged over dinner and we shared. All the child raising and crud detail—the baton twirling classes, the orthodontist, car pools, shopping, and errands—were mine alone.

It was no coincidence that I was giving voices to a lot of women through the column who were dealing with ambivalent feelings about themselves and their lives. I liked having a second career, but the price tag was exorbitant. Was it too much to ask that the men we had stood behind and supported all these years would do the same for us?

I watched these women—their pantyhose cutting them in half—as they dragged into my lectures to grab two hours for themselves before they had to make the car pool runs or meet the school buses. Before they got there they had retrieved a fork from the disposer, taken the dog to the vet, delivered a forgotten school lunch, dragged the garbage cans to the curb, dropped the lawn mower off at the shop for repairs, and accepted a garage full of Girl Scout cookies for distribution.

How long would it be before having a husband who made coffee in the mornings would no longer be enough?

"Bless Me Everybody for I Have Sinned"

⁂

You weren't supposed to count the number of people ahead of you in the line outside the confessional or keep track of how long they spent inside the shadowy cubicle, but everyone did it.

You were supposed to face the altar with your hands folded and your head bowed and look pious. When you heard a shuffling noise, you sorta backed up slowly. I looked at my watch. Four minutes! Who was in there? Father Andrew Greeley who had just written another explicit sex novel? My mind focused on how I could consolidate all of my failings and save a little time. Let's see, I could lump

together a group of sins under "irritability."
That would take in all the times I had lost my
temper and used the name of the Lord in vain.
I would follow this with "impatience." Yes,
impatience would make him forget irritability.
Who *was* that person in there still on his or
her knees? An ax murderer? An embezzler? Oh
God, please don't let it be a woman who said
no to her husband's sexual advances.

Father Frieder's confessional line was
shorter, but no one wanted to confess to
Father Frieder. He always asked questions
and gave you a sermon. Father Kelly had no
curiosity about details. He just wanted to get
out on the tennis court.

The blue curtain parted and a young
matron in slacks, wearing no makeup, emerged.
A small child rushed and slapped her leg and
yelled, "Where have you been? You said we'd
have a Slushee. I want to go."

That explained it.

The Catholic Church invented guilt. It
flowed like holy water, and every day women
bathed in it. We were like tourists trying to
buy something in a foreign country. We just
held our lives in both of our hands and invited
merchants to "take what you want."

"Bless Me Everybody for I Have Sinned"

If there was a bent fork that was mutilated by the disposer, we took it. If we fried an egg and the yolk broke, we assumed it was ours. If the first car stopped running, it became our car.

We gave the lean ham to our husbands, the front seat in the car to our mothers, the last piece of pizza to our children.

It is small wonder the offspring we gave birth to became the "me" generation. Something happens to a child who sees a mother pass up a dental checkup to buy a wardrobe for a Barbie doll who is going to an Ohio State football game with Ken over the weekend.

They are stigmatized by a martyred mother who cuts her own hair and pays $3 an hour for her daughter to learn how to throw a baton and break every lamp in the house.

Guilt is as old as dirt. It comes from the old proverb, "To Enjoy Is to Sin." In a marriage, you'd think the guilt could be divided, shared, but instead, marriage seems to compound guilt. Besides, women embrace it like a long lost lover.

Those who blazed trails on the march to equality by working outside the home paid a price for it . . . literally.

Erma Bombeck

For abandoning their children with a baby-sitter, $2,000 worth of toys, an electronic mecca, and enough soft drinks and snacks to feed a third world had to be offered up.

For missing a play or football game, the tab for guilt was hosting a party for two hundred sexually active teenagers on Saturday night.

If you didn't help your child with homework and he flunked English or you did help him with homework and he flunked math, the debt could go as high as a trip to Disneyland.

The reality was that families were faced with new mothers who were breaking some old rules. Instead of receiving support, their actions were challenged by those around them.

Their mothers said, "If you can stand to see your child run to a twelve-year-old baby sitter when he is hurt and in need of comfort, go ahead and get a job."

Their children charged, "I threw up today and you weren't home."

Even husbands, in their own subtle way, opened the refrigerator door and prodded, "How long are you going to save a peach pit in a two-quart mixing bowl?" (Tempting the reply, "Till hell freezes over!")

For a job that had no description and no

one waiting in line for it, it was ironic that a lot of women were secretly wondering, "Who do I have to sleep with to get fired from this job?"

I discovered something else about guilt in the '60s. There were exceptions. If you spent time away from your family delivering thirty empty egg cartons for the Christmas bazaar project or volunteering for playground duty, you were exempt from guilt.

However, if you held down a part-time job somewhere that took you out of the house for a few hours, you were pursuing your selfish interests and were a bad mother.

The operative word here seemed to be "money." If you got paid for something, it was bad for the children.

Guilt over careers outside the home wasn't the only form that plagued women of the '60s. The old nocturnal headache, an excuse for not having sex that had been passed down to us from our mothers, no longer played. Women no longer heeded their mothers' advice to "Grit your teeth and the whole mess will be over in a couple of years." They had begun to enjoy sex and felt guilty about that too.

In fact, remorse for not having the same priorities as their parents was a big thing with this generation. They never turned their mattresses from one year to the other, never cut up their own chickens to save money, and only ironed the backs of their husband's shirts if he planned on sweating and taking his jacket off.

As the decade wore on, guilt was headed for glut proportions. More men would come home to cold stoves. Children would have their own keys to open the door to an empty house. Grandparents would leave messages in the dust on the coffee tables. Father Kelly's tennis game would fall apart.

And it would be all my fault.

1967

Big-Time Guilt

❧

Forget the fact there were enough candles on my cake to light up a runway at O'Hare Airport. So I was forty. Did I care that all my contemporaries threw themselves into vats of Oil of Olay? To me, age was an attitude. You are as old as you feel. The Pope said that . . . or maybe it was Paul Harvey.

My life was going well. How could I be depressed? In two months, my first book would be published. The publisher was sending me on a book tour of Columbus, Cincinnati, and Cleveland, and I was even going to New York to be on *The Tonight Show*.

Besides, age just wasn't that important to

me. It wasn't the number of years you lived your life; it was what you did with those years. What were a few wrinkles? Badges of courage for living. You can only stay young by being active, I always said. Sit down and your feet swell. That was my philosophy. February 21 was just another day in my life.

February 21!

Wait a minute; it couldn't be. I grabbed a calendar. I was six weeks overdue. I numbed as the reality set in. I was an old woman who barely had time to feed herself and I was going to have a baby!

No, wait. It was probably menopause. That was it. I'd have a few meltdowns . . . yell at the dog . . . and . . . I was feeling a little queasy. Who was I kidding? It wasn't menopause. I was pregnant. I wanted to make my mark as a writer. Instead I was going to be remembered as the oldest woman in North America to give birth.

I would end up in the *Guinness Book of World Records* next to Josimar Carbauba of Brazil, who had thirty-eight children—the last one when she was fifty-four years old— or in the same paragraph with Ruth Kistler, who gave birth to a daughter in 1946 when she was forty-seven years and 129 days old.

It wasn't the idea of a child. I loved children.

Big-Time Guilt

It wasn't even the prospect of having something interfere with my career. I could write with swollen ankles.

The timing was all wrong.

When the kid outgrew naps, I'd be taking them.

When he was ready for a temporary driving permit, I'd be popping estrogen and trying to figure out whether my deafness was caused by the car radio or by deterioration.

When I was going to bed, he would be going out; when I got up, he'd be going to bed.

He'd amuse himself in the car on vacations by connecting liver spots on my hands.

I'd give him a graduation party with my Medicare check.

There are few moments in a woman's married life when she feels totally alone. Approaching motherhood at age forty is one of them.

The first thought that crossed my mind surprised even me. "Who can I pay to tell my mother?"

Selfishly, I came back to me. It wasn't fair. All my friends were moving on. They had burned their maternity clothes behind them like bridges. They had gone on diets, put their highchairs at the curb for Salvation

Army to claim, and gone in debt over their heads. The batteries had died on their biological clocks. What did I have to look forward to? Lamb-stained bibs, sleepless nights, Girl Scout cookies, Show and Tell, car pools, field trips, fevers at midnight. Their conversation would be full of sex therapist Dr. Reuben. Mine would be Dr. Spock.

After nine years of freedom, I was out of practice, out of patience, and out of the mood. I did not want a baby at age forty.

Then a sobering realization hit me. This wasn't just "my baby." It was "our baby." Bill had a stake in this and he was forty years old too. Of course, he would feel the same as me. There would probably be a lot of doubts going through his mind when I told him. Would he have to postpone his mid-life crisis to sit cross-legged at a Scouts powwow? Would the kid borrow his clothes for a nostalgia party at the dorm while he was still wearing them? When he explained sex to his teenage son, would he have to lecture from notes?

I felt better already. If we could cling to one another, we could get through it together. Not for a minute did I consider abortion. I just wanted someone to feel sorry for me and suffer with me. I knew this man so well. He would be just as disappointed about this pregnancy as I was. Besides, his concern for me having a baby at my age would probably draw us closer together.

I told him one night after dinner just after the kids had split to go wherever it is they go when there are dirty dishes, "I am pregnant."

"That's great!" he said excitedly. "When?"

"You don't have to pretend to be happy," I said.

"Who's pretending?" he smiled. "I'm thrilled to death. We're going to have another disciple."

"Bill, you're not listening. I'm forty years old," I reminded him.

"Forty is nothing," he gushed.

"If I were a tree in a national park, you could drive a car through me."

"Nonsense. Have you told the kids? They are going to be so excited. Especially Betsy. She's always after you to have a baby brother or sister."

"Betsy gets excited when she doesn't have to split a whole Pepsi with her brothers."

"Honey, I know it's a lot of work and it's nothing we planned," he said gently, "but the kids will help." (The kids had the attention span of gnats.) "Besides," he added, "a baby will keep us young."

Erma Bombeck

Right. I was only six weeks overdue and already I looked older than the pyramids.

The pregnancy continued. The nausea, the swollen ankles, the exhaustion. But inside something important was beginning to happen as it has to women since the beginning of time. Life was forming and, in a few months, we were bound together so closely there was no definite line between where I began and the child ended.

This didn't mean I was ready to give up on my S and S (Suffering and Sacrifice), but I was beginning to mellow and adjust. There were, after all, a few bright spots. I could use the same stretch marks and didn't have to lay new tracks. I had baby clothes by the boxes. I didn't have to suck in my stomach anymore.

In my fourth month, I sensed things were not going well. I didn't feel good, was extremely tired, and frankly didn't feel or look very pregnant.

My obstetrician voiced his concern and thought we should terminate the pregnancy. At that moment, I realized I had never wanted this baby more. I wasn't ready to give up on it. "Give it a few more months," I begged. I knew the life inside of me would begin to move.

Big-Time Guilt

For the next few months I did a lot of thinking about life and did a lot of bargaining with God. God doesn't deal.

In my sixth month, I had lost weight and was barely able to drag myself around. I was carrying a dead fetus.

I lost the baby.

The personal pronoun is important here. It is always, "We are going to have a baby," but when it comes down to the termination of a pregnancy, it's always the mother who confesses, "I lost it."

As I lay there mumbling "I am so sorry," the guilt was unbearable. Feelings of self-recrimination came and went like waves of nausea. I wanted that baby. Why hadn't I told anyone?

I had received a gift and had said, "I don't want it." In our marriage, it was just another lesson in sensitivity and forgiveness.

For me, it was to be the last time I would feel a miracle stirring within me. I had now joined a group of women who had to give a child back. They look like other women and they function like other women. But there is an emptiness inside of them that never goes away. At any given time of year when no one knows what they are talking about, they will look wistful and remark that the baby would

Erma Bombeck

be three years old today, or five, or ten. They play with the probabilities . . . the would have beens . . . could have beens . . . should have beens . . . and forever question, "Why?"

The Fixer-Upper

Lying in the darkness, Bill and I were as far apart from one another as we could get in a double bed.

We had not spoken to one another in two days.

I personally had no plans to speak to him for the rest of my life. I think my last words to him were, "I wouldn't spit on you if you were on fire!"

The word divorce was not mentioned. We were both afraid of getting custody of this lousy house we had just bought.

In the ad it was touted as "Gracious home steeped in history; a fixer-upper for the weekend handyman." It was like a dream come true. Located between two cemeteries, it was surrounded by twenty acres of trees and trails and a fenced-in polo field. Along the winding drive, there was a swimming pool bordered by a small scenic pond with a footbridge leading up to the house.

From a distance, the tall white pillars looked like Tara and encompassed a veranda porch. Inside were eleven rooms and five baths.

It was a house from hell.

When I first set eyes on it, I grabbed Bill and cried with childlike innocence, "Can we buy it, please?" What I should have been asking was, "Is the car in both names? Can we get an annulment after nineteen years of marriage? Could a forty-one-year-old woman with veins in the back of her knees wear heels and date again?"

Naturally, he was suspicious. Men are like that whenever women are happy.

"The house was built in 1840," I gushed.

"The plumbing is original," he said.

"Try to imagine it with a hillside of daffodils."

"The ground around the side porch is squishy and it smells."

"The high ceilings have such charm."

"There are enough mouse droppings in the attic to fertilize Costa Rica," he said.

The Fixer-Upper

"And those old trees lining the road look like a postcard."

"The potholes in the driveway are big enough for a car to fall through. It needs work."

I saw the wide-planked oak floors and the cute powder room off the entranceway.

He saw the water spots on the ceiling, 1/8-inch plumbing, and floors that squeaked and moved under his weight.

I cashed in every bit of femininity I had and begged, "C'mon. We could fix it up together. It'll be fun. The kids can help."

I don't think I've said anything as ridiculous since I told our children that when they grew up they would thank us for being so strict.

The kids acted like we had sentenced them to a penal institution and wanted no part of our projects. When we started something, I wanted it finished—sometime in my lifespan. Bill just wanted to come home each night and be Mister Rogers padding around in his soft shoes and saying wise things.

The latest confrontation had been over the kitchen wallpaper. I told him he was hanging the grapes upside down. He said I should just shut up and add some water to the paste.

Erma Bombeck

I said Adolf Hitler was a wallpaper hanger and he turned into a dictator too. Besides, there were a lot of bubbles he had missed that needed brushing out.

He said there wouldn't be any bubbles if the paste weren't so thick.

I told him from here on in he could take his own clothes to the cleaners.

He said he didn't know what that had to do with hanging wallpaper.

I said he was just like his mother, who ruined our wedding by wearing a black arm-band around her sleeve.

He said he hated the wallpaper when we bought it.

I said this is the kind of taste you'd expect from a man who is so insensitive that he refuses to put the car seat close to the pedals for me when he gets out of the car.

Then he really hurt. He said Michelangelo was married to a shrew like me. He wanted a nice, clean, white ceiling in the Sistine Chapel, but no, his wife wasn't happy until he had to lie on his back for three and a half years and paint a fresco.

It had been this way since the first day when we returned from the lumberyard with a piece of plywood two feet wider than a traffic lane and four feet longer than our car. We

The Fixer-Upper

had balanced it on the car roof. Bill held it in place by driving with his right hand and hanging onto the plywood with his left. It was my job to kneel on the seat, hang my head out of the car window like a carsick dog, and support the other side.

It gets worse. The dining room table held a rented sander. The bathtub was filled with bags of cement. Drop cloths and paint cans were everywhere.

We'd have saved a lot of time if we had just endorsed our checks over to the lumberyard and asked for an allowance to live on.

Living daily like Peace Corps workers in a Third World country began to take its toll. We were sick of sleeping in beds lined with crumbling plaster, brushing dust off chairs before guests could sit down, finding slivers of wood shavings in our food, and inhaling paint fumes from one month to the next. This wasn't a home. It was an unfinished symphony —like the Atlanta airport or St. John the Divine Cathedral in New York City. It would never be completed.

"This is like pouring sand down a rat hole," Bill said one evening. "Besides, it's taking its toll on all of us. We don't laugh anymore. We don't play. We don't have a good time."

Erma Bombeck

"I know."

"Maybe we should hire some handyman from around here to pull all of this together for us. It'll take a little longer than a big-time contractor, but we'll have some control over it and go at our own pace."

Pace is the operative word here. Had Mr. Sluggard been in charge of building the pyramids, he would still be digging out the basement.

Three local men accompanied him every morning to our kitchen: Curly, Moe, and Larry. They came to work at 6:30 A.M. in bib overalls with toothpicks in their teeth. They ripped up something and left at 2 P.M.

We told them to start by remodeling the kitchen.

We entered the next morning to find the entire kitchen wall had been knocked out. Mr. Sluggard smiled and said, "We'll have this bay window in for you in a couple of days."

"Mr. Sluggard," I said, "it's November and there is snow on my toaster and in front of my sink. I don't think this was a wise time to knock out a wall."

"In the summer we get real busy," said Larry . . . or maybe it was Moe.

When the kids dragged themselves in to breakfast, they turned blue and said sleepily,

The Fixer-Upper

"Has Dad been messing with the thermostat again?"

"Just think," I smiled weakly, "one day all of this will be yours."

"You and Dad have done nothing but argue since we moved here," one of the kids groused. "We're too far out of the city to have any friends and we hate it."

They were right. We had a pool we had never swum in . . . we just fed it chemicals. We never fished in the pond . . . we just pulled weeds that created algae out of it. We gazed on a polo field carpeted with acres of grass that had to be mowed every week.

That's when we made a decision to buy each of the kids a horse.

The euphoria span of children for pets is approximately fifteen minutes . . . less if the animal weighs 1,500 pounds and steps on their feet. Kids will jump to the ceiling and promise to groom animals, feed them, put up with disgusting bodily functions, and dedicate their lives to making them comfortable. By day two, they will not remember the animal's name.

All three horses had the same things in common: their faces sucked up food and water like a minesweeper; they looked like a postcard from Churchill Downs; and they had this little quirk about anyone sitting on their backs. They didn't permit it.

Our friends thought the property was like Disneyland. Only we knew the truth. The house exhausted us. Every time we turned around, something else needed attention. The fruit trees in the orchard were dying because of some strange weevil that bored holes in the fruit. The grass turned brown. The pond turned to green slime and smelled. The furnace made strange sounds when it clicked on. The driveway needed to be plowed to remove snow before we could get to the front door.

I promised Bill things would be better between us when we no longer had to sit around the breakfast table in parkas. They weren't. Mr. Sluggard finished with the bay window and moved on to the dining room. As we sat in the kitchen having dinner one night, we heard something scratching behind the baseboard. Not a small scratch but a large one. I mentioned it to Mr. Sluggard, who laughed and said, "I plumb forgot to board up a small hole in the outside wall. Probably a few rats got in."

"Rats!" I gasped. "There are rats in my woodwork?"

"They're not hurting anything," he said. "That's how they sharpen their teeth."

The Fixer-Upper

I wanted to hurt Mr. Sluggard.

"How do we get them out?" I asked evenly.

"I wouldn't bother with it," he said. "They'll eventually die."

I could always predict when a rat would die in the woodwork. It would wait until we had company. We were giving a dinner party for a dozen people one night. Guests were gathered around an antique organ in the living room, singing, when one of them started to smell her drink and clutched her throat. "What's that smell?" she gasped.

"What does it smell like?" I asked.

"Raw sewage."

"I'll check dinner," I said and made a quick exit.

The house brought home something very significant in our marriage. We discovered we were totally incompatible. We couldn't do anything together. Whenever I wanted a nail driven in the wall to hold a picture, I would tell Bill I needed a hole drilled and prepare to grow old. By the time he brought in his entire inventory of drills and bits, his stud finder, tape measure, and ladders, I had lost interest.

When he painted anything he had an annoying habit of washing his brushes out afterward instead of soaking them in a coffee can until they turned stiff and died.

Erma Bombeck

I hated spending money on things that didn't show. My philosophy was to fill the flower beds with geraniums and if we had to wait three hours for the bathtub to fill, who cared?

We never said hello anymore. I'd meet him at the end of the driveway and whine, "Did you bring the caulking gun?" or "Something with wings is hatching in the basement. Take a look before dinner."

As he was writing checks one Friday night, he said, "Do you realize Mr. Sluggard and his comedy team have been with us for three years?"

"Seems longer," I said.

"Are you happy?" he asked suddenly.

"Compared to what?"

"Compared to people who don't have to carry water or shower with a vegetable spray."

"What are you really asking?" I said.

"Why don't we unload this house and get on with our lives?"

A house is like a car. You can't talk in front of it or it will punish you. If either of these inanimate objects knows you are going to dump it, it will turn on you. If it is a car, the transmission will fall out, all four tires will go bald, or it will crash itself into a tree.

The Fixer-Upper

Our house reacted as if it was starring in a Stephen King movie. Every day, something struck back. Our realtor told us we would have to show that the property was in good running order. Samples of our pond water (which we used for showers and laundry) tested at high levels of arsenic. Since our well could not supply water for the entire house, we had to hire a water witch to walk across the back forty and wait for his divining rod to quiver. With each bump-bump of the drill, I heard fifty cents . . . fifty cents . . . fifty cents . . . for four solid days and nights before we struck a new vein of water.

While the pond was being checked, the inspector smelled gas. The line that ran the three-quarters of a mile to the road needed to be replaced as it had deteriorated. We did that.

The realtor said someone was sure to notice the smell in the side yard, so we had the septic tank replaced.

Also, the one furnace was hopelessly inadequate for such a large house and a new one had to be added to attract buyers. And no one would consider living in it unless all those chimneys were tuck pointed to stop the leaks.

The new owners were young and ecstatic

over their fixer-upper. "It's going to be such fun," they chirped.

I had some guilt as we pulled out of the driveway. They would need the services of an exorcist to rid the house of Mr. Sluggard.

After twenty-two years of marriage, we had outgrown the challenge of making something out of nothing. The nesting instincts just weren't there anymore. I no longer hyperventilated over a melon keeper that I bought at a Tupperware party. I now worshiped at the shrine of convenience and Sara Lee. Bill no longer rushed home to make bird houses in the basement. He wanted to sleep in his BarcaLounger so he wouldn't be so tired when he went to bed.

It was as if we were closing the door on the years of struggle. It wasn't fun anymore.

Before moving on to a new life in Arizona, we took a vacation. In our travels, we stopped off at Monticello in Virginia to visit the home of Thomas Jefferson.

Just inside the front door, the guide asked those of us on the tour to note the unusual clock that Mr. Jefferson had designed and installed. It was a unique timepiece in that on one side of the door a weight rose with each second as another went down on the other side. Since Mr. Jefferson had miscalculated the time it took the weights to complete their journey, he had to cut a hole in the floor to accommodate the clock.

As I stared into the large, ugly hole in the entranceway of this beautiful mansion, I whispered to Bill, "Was he married?"

Bill whispered back, "Not happily."

Creative Arguing

———— ✿ ————

When married couples say "We never argue,"
it's an incomplete sentence. "We never argue
in public/in front of the children/during sex,"
maybe. But there is something wrong with
two people who agree to never disagree.

Psychologists who study this kind of
behavior say that certain kinds of fights can
actually improve some marriages. It gives
mates a chance to express their anger and
perhaps learn how to compromise when
there are differences.

I can say without a shred of modesty that
I became quite good at expressing anger.
How? Practice, practice, practice.

Creative Arguing

I have engaged in some of the most dazzling wars of words ever spoken in anger. The fact that I have remained married is nothing short of a miracle. These arguments are not for amateurs. Do not try them in your own home. I use them only as examples of how creative you can get.

The Nocturnal Confrontation. You have just climbed into bed. Your husband is feeling romantically inclined. He kisses your ear and cups your face in his hands tenderly. You whisper, "Why are you being so stubborn about the new slipcovers?"

There is nothing that takes the passion out of a man like writing a check just before he reaches for his wife.

Another risky argument in the same arena is the "I cannot make love with a mosquito in the bedroom." After Bill chased this pest one night for thirty minutes, he trapped it in the bathroom and considered it a kill. When he finally squashed it, I ragged him for two hours about animal rights.

Kids serve as great battlefields for arguments. Disagreeing over one's children isn't much of a challenge, however, as the odds of a mother and father loving all of their children at the same time on a given day are nil.

Political Differences are good. I love these

election-year altercations because you can chew on them for the next four years. Every time your garbage isn't picked up or you find a piece of glass in your taco, you can blame it on your husband (or wife), who voted for the Neanderthal in the White House in the first place.

High-Risk arguments are fun. This one is inspired. One Super Bowl day, I decided to rearrange the furniture and vacuum. Don't try this one without witnesses.

In all fairness, my husband has brought some creativity to arguments. The one that brings instant response is: I Am Not Lost. We could be surrounded by 15,000 head of cattle and drive through three time zones and he would not admit he has no idea where he is.

The Phantom Critic always gets a rise out of me. It's a nonverbal argument. Following my naps, I always feel the need to hike the thermostat up. As I reached up one afternoon to spin the dial I saw a note attached to it. It read, "Sleep-induced body temperature declines are not uncommon. Usually the body temperature returns to normal within minutes of resumption of normal activity. Normal activity does not include hiking thermostat up." It was signed "Mr. Science."

These examples, of course, are for professionals. Neophytes would do well to start off with simple disagreements. For example, your husband hates broccoli. He throws up at the sight of it. If you sneak broccoli into the house, he knows it. He has instructed you never to cook it. You go to a dinner party where a hostess in a tight cashmere sweater puts broccoli in front of him and he not only scarfs it down, he says, "Honey, why don't you get her recipe for broccoli."

Then you can work your way up to his Talking Down to You attacks. "Put your fork in the toaster before unplugging it and you will never need another hair appointment as long as you live."

The arguments I like are the ones that have an extended life. You know, the ones that not only get two people going, but seduce other members of the family into them.

The confrontation that put our marriage on the cutting edge of separation was over the bread machine.

We had gotten my mother one for Christmas. She is a woman who cannot assemble a box and she made bread in the bread machine.

As I dumped flour into the appliance, I felt a presence at my elbow. "Aren't you going to walk your way through the manual first?" asked Bill. (He considered manuals right up there with the Dead Sea Scrolls.)

"I'm not walking anywhere. Get me a cup of water."

He slammed down the lid, nearly crushing my fingers. "Wait a minute! What are you going to do about those digital pads?"

"I'm going to press the one that says START," I said defiantly.

"You are going to do nothing of the sort. You don't even know when to add the yeast."

"I've got news for you, Mr. Pillsbury Doughboy with an attitude, I've already added the yeast."

I pushed the button. A red light went on. He actually turned pale. "You don't have a clue what is going on in there," he charged. "Would it kill you to read instructions first?"

We sniped at one another for three hours. One of our sons came into the kitchen just as the beep sounded indicating the bread was finished.

I lifted the lid and my son and I inhaled the smell of yeast. As I turned the loaf out on a towel, part of it clung to the sides of the unit. My son grabbed a knife and began to pry the sides loose.

"I don't believe you people," shouted my

husband. "Two more signatures and I could put both of you away. It says right here in the manual you are never to use a sharp instrument to loosen the bread from the receptacle as it will scratch the surface." I fought the impulse to load my salad shooter with carrots and let him have it between the eyes.

"Dad," said our son, "it's coming loose."

"That's what I'd expect from someone who puts Gatorade in a boiling radiator."

Now there were two of us involved.

Later, when the story was repeated to my mother, she said, "Erma's right. There's nothing to it."

This little argument was on its way to becoming a line drawn in the sand that would forever affect relationships. You either believed in reading instructions for the bread machine—or you didn't. You couldn't be neutral.

My personal favorite, however, is the No Argument. I wouldn't give Bill a hint as to what I was angry about. Every time he asked why, I would look him directly in the eyes and say, "*You* know." After a while he began to believe he knew. He said "I'm sorry" and promised never to do again what he didn't know he had done in the first place.

Experts contend that healthy fights

develop a kind of marital efficacy that makes marriage stronger as time goes on. You just have to know when to disagree, how far to go, and how to keep anger within bounds.

For example, I never bring up the words "bread machine" around the holidays. It could ruin the entire season for everyone.

1971

Teenagers

At a time in our marriage when everything should have come together, Bill and I were floundering in a sea of disharmony, unable to communicate with one another and living at the poverty level.

That is because we were being held captive by three teenagers. They were everywhere. They sequestered themselves behind locked doors that reverberated with whining guitars that made your teeth itch and caused chest pains. They stood like concrete statues in front of the open refrigerator waiting for something to move. They used towels like nose tissue and shampoo like it flowed from a spigot. The phone served as an umbilical cord—sever it and they turned pale. They got an allowance for breathing.

It had been different when they were small. There were rules and when these rules were broken, there were favors that were withheld. Now, we were clearly outnumbered three to two.

Not only had we lost control over them, we had lost all sense of ourselves. We didn't know who we were anymore. Every day with teenagers is like the final two days of a five-year pregnancy. Every day you wake up asking, "When is it going to end?"

You reach the point where you can no longer remember what it was like to use a toilet without flushing it *first,* or to have a bunch of bananas that lasted longer than fifteen minutes.

Secretly, the two of us made plans to reclaim the turf that was rightfully ours. We were going to slip out into the living room one night and capture the remote control so we could watch what we wanted on TV, but that never panned out.

We were going to plan an evening without checking to see if we could use our own car, but that didn't happen either.

It had been a long time since Bill and I were alone. Luckily, we were two people who wanted the same things.

Teenagers

As I readied for bed one night, I yelled out to Bill, who was cutting his toenails, "Remember the fun we used to have rearranging furniture? I'm going to make some changes when the kids move out."

"You know what I've been thinking," he yelled back. "I'd like to go back to school for my Ph.D."

"Maybe you could put in a vegetable garden so we could putter around in it. That's something we could do together."

"I've always liked administration and I could go farther with a degree," he said.

"Your BarcaLounger has to go. I know you like it, but I'd like something in chintz."

"You know what else?" he said excitedly. "When the kids are gone I'm going to get myself in an exercise program. What I'd really like to do," he said, "is get in good enough shape to run the Boston Marathon."

"Maybe you could put some new shutters in the living room. Those big wide ones. You used to love to paint."

"I figure if I bought a motorcycle we could do with one less car. I could tool around the campus and back. Maybe grow a beard. I've always wanted to grow a beard."

I stood in the doorway of the bathroom looking at him. "What did you say?"

"I said maybe I'd grow a beard to go with the motorcycle."

Who was this man? Certainly not the one I married twenty-two years ago in Dayton, Ohio.

Could Laura Ashley find happiness with the Easy Rider? He was going in one direction and I was going in the other.

"I was hoping we might get season tickets to the Symphony," I said.

"I was hoping we could do a little traveling," he said.

We both crawled into bed and he turned off the light.

I stared into the darkness. What if those three eating machines we were raising were all we had in common after all these years? What if we awoke one morning and discovered we didn't laugh at the same things, cry at the same things, or care about the same things?

So much of our energies had been focused on family, we had had little time for one another. Could we let go and find we still had something left upon which to build?

How did we perceive these three human beings who impacted on our lives? Were they pets that we owned and toilet trained to be socially acceptable? Little creatures that we gave food and lodgings and whose shots we updated? Did we teach them to run and fetch, sit and heel, and reward them for patience and loyalty?

Or were they like appliances with a lifetime warranty that were there to serve us like a toaster?

Sometimes we acted like they were endowments that we had put down hard cash for and from which we expected rich dividends at their maturity. These investments were supposed to sustain us in our declining years.

Some parents perceived their children as used cars that they kept running and got rid of when they started to cost money.

Still others regarded their children as mirrors that reflected their image in every way. And then one day when they looked at the mirror and saw a flaw, a crack, or a distorted view—something other than their own image—they discarded them and chalked their lives up to failure.

How did Bill and I see our children? Were they a safety net for our marriage? When either of us stopped talking to cach othcr . . . did we go to them? Did we use them for personal triumphs instead of one another? Did we involve ourselves in their lives to keep from living our own?

I broke the silence. "Bill, how do you see our children?"

"Rarely," he grunted.

"I see them as kites," I said. "You spend a lifetime trying to get them off the ground. You run with them until you're both breathless . . . they crash . . . you add a longer tail . . . they hit the rooftop . . . you pluck them out of the spouting . . . you patch and comfort, adjust and teach. You watch them lifted by the wind and assure them that someday they'll fly."

Bill flipped on the light and stared at me in disbelief.

"Finally, they are airborne," I continued, "but they need more string and you keep letting it out, and with each twist of the ball of twine there is a sadness that goes with the joy because the kite becomes more distant and somehow you know that it won't be long until that beautiful creature will snap the life-line that bound you together and soar as it was meant to soar . . . free and alone."

"Are you finished?" he finally said.

"Yes."

"Because one of your kites just hit the center garage post and he only has a $100 deductible!"

The Sexual Revolution

✿

It was a bad week. The rubber broke in the elastic waistband of my favorite slacks. The power went off and I lost everything in the freezer. A story in the newspaper said that marriage was going out of style.

Well, didn't that just put the frosting on the cake. After serving nearly a quarter of a century in this institution called marriage, it was now passé. It's like cleaning an oven the day before it catches fire.

Most of us in the neighborhood were hanging tough, but already news of divorces had begun to circulate from people who had racked up a lot of years together. The very thought of infidelity titillated us. We had all read *Diary of a Mad Housewife* and devoured the advice columns—especially the one telling about a woman who set down rules on what to do if a married man had a heart attack in your apartment while making love to you. She was as cool and clinical about it as if she was listing instructions on how to get the rust out of your steam iron.

The only one of us who had ever come close to an indiscretion was Cindy. Her butcher leaned over one day and whispered, "Are you ready for a tryst?"

Cindy thought he said "trip" and shouted back, "Not until the last two weeks in August when Ed gets his vacation."

When someone asked me once if I ever thought of leaving Bill, I asked, "Where?"

Outwardly, we seemed smug and secure about our marriages. Inside, there was a nagging feeling that the winds blowing across the plains of suburbia were bringing changes to our lives. The roads into the cities were being traveled by more and more women who were working outside of the home. The farmlands were dotted with fast food emporiums. Those of us who stayed at home and resisted minimum wages had only one figure who could lead us out of the

wilderness into the twenty-first century—
Phil Donahue.

He lived across the street from us for
about five years, and I watched his career
rise to national attention. Phil was everyone's husband, the husband who might not
always understand the problem, but was willing to listen. He was honest and open and his
TV show provided us with a menu of person-
alities who challenged us to think. He was
one of the first men to publicly play to the
intelligence of women on the home front and
say, "You're better than you think you are."

We were all glued to the TV set the morning in 1973 when a pretty, blonde Florida
housewife, Marabel Morgan, appeared on
Phil's show to guide us back to the road of
sanity where she thought we belonged . . . a
magical place with picket fence and tie-back
curtains . . . a place where we could become
the title of her book, *The Total Woman*.

Marabel was touted to be an antidote for
the madness that prompted wives to leave
their husbands and children and to pursue
their own ambitions outside the home.

"What would your husband see if he
came home within the next ten minutes?" she
charged. "Are there dirty dishes in the sink
and a vacuum cleaner in the living room? Are

you dowdy and overweight and wearing faded culottes and sneakers without socks?"

"The woman's an oracle," said Helen.

Marabel continued. "Stop nagging your husband and accept him as he is."

"Get outta here," I mumbled.

"Tonight when he comes home, concentrate on his body, really look at him and see him through another woman's eyes . . . his secretary's or your neighbor's. Tell him how you've thought of nothing all day but his body."

By the time Marabel had described making love in a bathtub of Jell-O and wearing nothing but Saran Wrap to meet him at the door, we not only stopped scarfing down doughnuts, we stopped breathing. Never before had we heard sex talked about so openly.

The practical thing to do was to write Marabel off as a *Stepford Wives* throwback, but in each of us a bell went off . . . a warning that said marriage could no longer be taken for granted.

More couples than ever were saying "I do," but they said it more often.

According to statistics, 50 percent of marriages were ending in divorce. Of that number 60 percent remarried within five years. About three-quarters of these went on to marry for a third and fourth time. The most popular diet of the '70s was a divorce and 500 calories a day.

By the beginning of the next decade, it was estimated 14 million women would be sharing the same husband, same kids, same friends, same paycheck, and mutual stress.

Some of our friends were splitting after long marriages. I asked one of them, "What advice would you give to your former husband's new wife?" She said, "Just three words, 'Don't grow old.'"

Another one said, "I'd probably offer to pay her child support. She just took a fifty-two-year-old teenager off my hands."

Along with the anger and bitterness I witnessed another dimension: equation families. A whole brother and two half-sisters divided by two mothers (one step) equals a whole father, plus a weekend dad, divided by seven grandparents (subtract two who have died) including two others who have remarried and multiplied.

My kids brought a story home of a teacher who came across the same last name of two students and asked, "Are you twins?"

"No," said one, "we were born three months apart."

"Then you are half-brothers?"

Erma Bombeck

The other one said, "I'm not sure. We have the same father, but I live with the second mother and he lives with the third mother."

His half-brother commented, "It was easier when we were cousins."

Could we afford to be complacent? Was it possible someone was out there lusting for a man whose idea of excitement was having his soup served hot?

You had to be blind not to notice that whenever second wives appeared at a function, the dinosaur wives put on fresh lipstick and closed ranks.

You couldn't miss the second stringers. They were half their husbands' ages, often several inches taller, had visible hipbones, and were accomplished in their own right. As they nibbled on ears and stared into eyes, they were dedicated to dispel the notion that men peaked sexually at age eighteen.

In some ways I envied the trophy wives. There seemed to be that look between them and their spouses that said, "Let's go home." We had that once. Each listened attentively while the other spoke. We had not only heard one another's stories, we needed each other to finish them. They had children and homes and jobs to look forward to. That was all behind us.

The Sexual Revolution

But we couldn't help but look at our husbands, a little paunchy around the middle, a little bald on the top, a little slow in the step, and reflect, "Somewhere tonight, his new wife is being born."

I don't know if sex actually increased or if we were talking more openly about it. But everything was sexy from deodorant to breath mints, from toothpaste to cars. Films had changed. Censors who used to hyperventilate when one of the persons in bed did not have a foot on the floor (even Bambi couldn't conceive with those kinds of limitations) were ignored. Kissing not only became an aerobic exercise, it resembled someone scarfing down a late lunch. You couldn't pick up a newspaper or a magazine where people weren't singing like canaries about their sex lives.

We knew that more people make love on Sunday than any other day of the week. We knew that the peak hours are 10 P.M. to 7 A.M.

We knew that power outages led to an increase in the birthrate significantly nine months later.

We knew that more women sleep next to the wall than men.

We knew that men wearing boxer shorts are more likely to become fathers.

We knew that jogging increases sexual desires.

We knew that garlic is still the most effective form of birth control.

We knew that after sixty, sex is termed "interesting."

We knew that we burn 150 calories making love, which is just under how many are burned throwing a Frisbee to the dog.

We knew that the incidence of lovemaking runs from 7.4 times per week to as high as 9.64.

We weren't just learning things our mothers never told us . . . we were learning things our mothers didn't even know.

Probably the trend that bothered me the most was the theory television advanced . . . that when TV couples marry—ratings decline.

The message went out loud and clear that there is no life after the marital bed. Keep the heroes and heroines teasing one another to death and you had an audience.

What they were saying was that marriage couldn't pull a 30 share. No one wanted to watch legalized sex anymore.

Were the best years behind us?

Buzz words on marriage filled the air like fireflies on a summer night. A good marriage needed "disclosure" where couples exchanged feelings about themselves. It needed "feed-back" that was positive and helpful to your partner, to let him know how you reacted to what he said. "Communication" became the cliché of the '70s. Someone figured out married people spoke to one another only thirty minutes a week. The reasons were laid at the feet of the fast-paced life we were leading, the disappearing dinner hour, and television.

I personally thought it was because we told all the good stuff the first week and then went into reruns . . . telling the same stories about relatives and childhood, nagging one another over the same faults, sharing the same complaints over the same children, and rehashing the same feelings.

It was just something to keep you stirred up. We were at a party one night when Marilyn said, "There isn't a day goes by that Charlie and I don't say something meaningful to one another. Meaningful conversations are important to the success of a marriage. In fact, if you don't have anything meaningful to say to one another, your marriage is not going to last."

As we drove home from the party I broke a fifteen-minute silence with, "Have we ever had a meaningful conversation?"

"I don't think so," Bill said.

We drove for another five miles or so

without speaking. Finally I said, "What is a meaningful conversation?"

"I'm not sure," he said.

"Then how do we know we didn't have one?"

"I think it's a conversation with meaning . . . like the oil embargo or Paul Harvey," he said.

"What about them?" I asked.

"What about who?"

"The oil embargo and Paul Harvey."

"It doesn't have to be about the oil embargo and Paul Harvey. It could be a discussion on anything that is pertinent."

"I cut my legs shaving yesterday."

"That's not pertinent to anyone but you."

"I used your razor. By the way," I added, "I called you at school the other day."

"Anything important?"

"Don't you remember? I told you to hurry home. I wanted your body."

"What did I say?"

"You put me on hold," I said icily.

The sexual revolution was to impact on the marriages of future generations. I dreaded the day when our children asked us what we did to aid in the advancement of sexual freedom.

Somehow I had the feeling that "I tried to give at the office" wouldn't win me a place in history.

1974

The Dinosaurs

━━━━━━━━ ❧ ━━━━━━━━

We looked a little ridiculous—two forty-seven-year-old adults sitting alone around a card table in the backyard with pointed party hats strapped under our chins.

Nearby, a smoking grill created a special hell in the Arizona August heat, which had already reached 113 degrees.

It wasn't the way I had imagined our twenty-fifth wedding anniversary gala.

When I fantasized about it, I visualized a large white tent housing a six-piece orchestra. The inside would be decorated with flowers and several hundred guests would be milling around. My husband and I would exchange matching diamond-studded tennis bracelets. He would romantically feed me blueberries out of season, and the orchestra would play our favorite song, "Our Love Is Here to Stay," while we swayed together on the dance floor.

Later, we would throw streamers from the second deck of a cruise ship and swill champagne while our misty-eyed children waved from the dock.

The reality was our kids had thrown a couple of hamburgers and a few hot dogs on the grill, scarfed them down and split, leaving us to clean up. The pool table nearby held our bounty: matching one-size-fits-all bathrobes and, from my husband, a shower booster with five positions ranging from gentle spray to pin-you-against-the-wall.

Twenty-five years. There had been a time when we would have gotten a standing ovation on *The Price Is Right* for being married that long. Not anymore.

Kids just looked at you like you were some kind of prehistoric animal with a brain incapable of supporting your body. Your contemporaries just shook their heads in disgust and whispered to one another, "She'd leave him in a minute, but she's too out of shape to shop."

The Dinosaurs

When I read the Sunday paper, I found myself turning frequently to the section of anniversaries ... people who had survived fifty or sixty years of marriage. In some strange way they were my future, sitting side by side, not touching, staring straight at the camera. Her hair was thin with a tinge of pink scalp showing through. So was his. Their jowls hung limp without a trace of a smile. They had wrinkles deep enough to plant a spring crop and were wearing matching glasses.

I knew it would only be a matter of time before Bill's beard was bits of white fuzz and I grew a mustache. No one would be able to tell us apart.

Already our ideas, our stories, our ideology, and our attitudes had blended to such a degree we barely knew where one began and the other one left off. Whenever he told the joke about the duck in the sauna, I knew the exact moment he was going to say, "Help me with the punchline, Honey."

And there was not another living soul who could make any sense out of what I was talking about when I told him about the "ping" in my car.

Mentally, I checked the list of the things I was going to change about him twenty-five years ago. He was still late all the time and still left-handed. He saw his cronies less . . . but had replaced them with other distractions like jogging and fishing. I threw him a vegetable or two every week and he was satisfied he was eating healthy. The burr haircut had grown out, but I had little to do with that. Actually, he had less hair to worry about.

I wondered for the first time if he had made such a list of my annoyances and what kind of progress he had made.

Bill scraped the last hamburger from the grill and asked, "You want this? If you don't, I'll throw it away."

The disposer gene in me kicked in and I popped it in my mouth.

"This was nice," he said.

"Did you know that Richard Burton bought Liz a rare diamond for their anniversary and she bought him a full-length fur coat?"

"What would I do with a fur coat in Phoenix in August?" he snorted.

I looked at him as he returned the folding chairs to their original boxes. We had gone through three wars, two miscarriages, five houses, three children, nine cars, twenty-three funerals, seven camping trips, twelve jobs, nineteen banks, and three credit unions.

The Dinosaurs

I had cut his hair, cleaned up his toenail clippings, and turned 33,488 pieces of his underwear right side out. He had washed my feet when I was pregnant and couldn't see them, bought feminine products for me when I couldn't get out of the house, and put his car seat back to its original position after I had used it 18,675 times.

We had shared toothpaste, debts, closets, and relatives. We had given one another honesty and trust. We had given our children something they weren't even aware of and took for granted . . . stability.

He came over to where I was seated and said, "I've got a present for you."

"What is it?" I asked excitedly.

"Something you like. Close your eyes."

When I opened them, he was holding a cauliflower that comes packed in a pickle jar.

"I hid it from the kids," he said, "because I know you like the cauliflower."

Maybe love was that simple.

Whatever Happened to Romance?

—————— ❧ ——————

You don't see it slipping away, but somewhere between wearing maternity underwear under a flannel nightgown to bed and receiving a salad spinner for Christmas, the romance fades.

You sense something is missing. The electric currents of passion that used to erupt when you passed one another in the hallway or the meltdown you felt when your hands touched as you exchanged notes are no longer there. You have the feeling your furniture communicates more than you do.

Not that I married romance, but women who read Barbara Cartland, had seen *Gone*

Whatever Happened to Romance?

With the Wind eight times, and fantasized over Paul Newman . . . lived in hope.

I didn't expect Bill to rent space on a billboard wishing me Happy Birthday or send me flowers on Groundhog Day, but giving me a pencil and pen set after the birth of our first child? Get real.

Romance was something women always talked about. How could a man be married to them all these years and not know them?

To the naked eye, I look like your basic no-nonsense, practical, down-to-earth wife and mother who turns to mush when she receives a cookie press that turns mashed potatoes into rosettes.

But behind the facade beats the heart of a tramp.

I always wanted the ultimate nightgown that Mr. Frederick puts in the show window or a jumpsuit made out of fake animal fur, preferably leopard or cheetah. I always wanted fingernails so long you couldn't make meat loaf with them and eight-inch-heel bedroom slippers that excited the cat.

I remember the Christmas I pushed back the tissue on a large box, my heart beating with excitement as I fantasized about a mink hat or a jacket.

My eyes fell on a miniature sixteen-inch-tall rustic table and two log chairs. Growing out of the table was an ear of dried corn. A small white trellis completed the setting.

"I give up," I said. "What is it?"

"Figure it out," Bill replied.

"Barbie and Ken are going Hee Haw?"

"No, no," he said, "think of nature."

"Barbie and Ken are fighting cholesterol."

"Does the word 'squirrel' have any meaning for you?" he asked.

"You'll never know how much," I said dryly.

"It's a squirrel feeder," he said excitedly.

A squirrel feeder. The Duke of Windsor on his anniversary flew from abroad to present the Duchess with thirty-eight flavors of her favorite ice cream.

Composer Adolph Green and his actress-wife, Phyllis Newman, received an arrangement of a love song, "Just in Time," as a gift from Leonard Bernstein.

My dentist rented the billboard next to McDonald's that proclaimed, "I love you, Eileen."

I got a squirrel feeder.

Sensing my disappointment, Bill said, "You've got everything."

When did I become a woman who had everything? It seemed ludicrous that someone who walked around with a pin in her underwear would have everything. What *do* you buy such a woman? Bath salts? I had enough of them to connect Miami to Key West with a sandy beach of bath crystals. No one ever considered the fact that I took showers.

Then I went through a period of practicality and became the gadget goddess. If Mommy loved the egg separator, she'd go nuts with a wooden board with three holes that measured the right amount of spaghetti to cook.

One Christmas a few years back, I advanced to "themes." I got nursing pigs on their backs that were really salt and pepper shakers, pig notepads, and pig potholders. The next Christmas, it was cats. Cat clocks, cat memo pads, cat calendars, cat sweaters, and cats that held recipes.

I even got a bird feeder that looked like a Western saloon and a ceramic armadillo filled with cashew nuts.

Can a marriage survive the gift of a water heater or a hitch for the trailer? Of course it can. There is no correlation between love and rewards. I told myself that Gloria's husband bought her a fur jacket for her birthday because he was fooling around with his dental hygienist.

There is a period, however, when wives

still have hopes of recapturing the intimacy that was once a part of their lives.

At a bookstore one day I picked up one of those softcover books that promise a surefire return to romance if you follow some of the author's suggestions.

I zipped through the part about spreading potpourri throughout the house and putting notes in his sandwich that said "I love you." (He'd just chew up the note and complain the sandwich was dry.)

I laughed through the section that advised us to climb into our red sports car with the top down and speed to our boat, where we would anchor each evening in a different cove.

But I did pay close attention to the intimate dinner by candlelight chapter. I could pull that off. It was a timetable for romance.

4:30 P.M. I set the table for two with wedding linens and candles. Clean the salad greens and chill salad plates and forks.

4:45 P.M. Slide chicken casserole in oven and chill wine. Retrieve iced tea spoons from bedrooms. Take dessert out of freezer and put in refrigerator to defrost.

5:00 P.M. Send kids to movie.

5:15 P.M. Pick hibiscus from bush in yard and arrange in brandy snifter in center of table. Take shower and cut toenails. Put perfume behind both knees.

5:30 P.M. Slow down chicken casserole and put vegetables in pan ready to heat up. Arrange rolls on cookie sheet. Load stereo with records and turn down lights.

6:00 P.M. Watch news. Put appetizer back in refrigerator. Return frozen dessert, which has turned into a beverage, to freezer.

7:00 P.M. Eat half sandwich and put foil over casserole, which is real brown. Discard hibiscus centerpiece, which has closed and died. Replace with fake poinsettia.

8:00 P.M. Hear car in driveway. Light candles, throw overcooked casserole in middle of table. Toss limp vegetables and frosted salad on husband's plate.

8:01 P.M. Husband enters house and says cheerily, "Hi Honey, I'm home."

I slouch in the chair and snap, "Shut up! Sit down! Eat!"

Women generally hang on to their illusions about romance. They want desperately to believe it's a phase men go through and that one day they will appear at the door with violets out of season, a bottle of wine, and two airline tickets to Paris.

"What are we celebrating?" you ask, putting down your toilet brush.

"Life!" he says, grabbing you around the waist. "I just wanted to say 'I adore you.'"

That will happen on the day two squirrels sit down at our picnic table feeder and order a corn-on-the-cob daiquiri.

For Better or for Work

The '70s was the era of illegible notes on the refrigerator door saying "I'll be late." It was a time when sex was listed on a memo pad under "Things to Do Today." Women ran around before dinner defrosting lamb chops under each arm.

The house that was supposed to return to normalcy when our three kids went off to college became a command center for dueling careers.

Could a marriage survive this frenzy? Who knew? The question had never been asked before. Women determined to become more than second-class citizens called it a revolution. Men, confused by all of the anger and equality, liked to refer to it as a virus.

We were breaking new ground in the American family, and there were things our mothers never told us because they had never lived in an egalitarian world.

Who gets custody of the checkbook?

Who takes out the garbage?

How do you keep from competing with one another?

Who gets the oil changed in the car?

Whose money is it? His? Mine? Ours?

Do we ask our husbands to set the table . . . or would it compromise their masculinity?

Should men ask their wives to sew a button on their shirts, or is this demeaning for an account executive who paid to have the house painted?

Should a woman play down her promotion and raise to keep her husband's self-esteem intact?

Should a husband brag about his wife's successes or would he sound condescending?

Who disciplines the children? Is it still "Wait till your father gets home" or is it now "Wait till your mother gets home"?

For twelve years I had been dinking around writing a syndicated column for a couple of hundred newspapers. I had published three books and signed on as a regular correspondent for a new morning show, *Good Morning America.*

None of it had changed my life significantly. I worked from my home, so it was no problem to stir the beans, start a load of laundry, or clean the oven in between writing and taping.

In 1976, I published a book called *The Grass Is Always Greener Over the Septic Tank.* It became a best-seller, increased my number of newspapers by several hundred, and catapulted me to national attention. There was a ten-week book tour during which I appeared on every talk show being aired. *Life* magazine profiled my family and me. I figured it was only a matter of time before men threw me their hotel keys in airports.

By all odds, this was the move that could have torn our marriage asunder.

There were three things that saved it. First, at age forty-nine, I didn't have the energy to maintain an ego. An ego needs daily inflating and constant grooming. Every day, the egotist rolls out of bed and takes his emotional temperature. Then he looks in a mirror and asks, "Am I as brilliant today as I was yesterday? Of course. But what about tomorrow?"

Second, I discovered I didn't enjoy notoriety very much. I loved to write but was shy and uncomfortable with the trappings that came with it.

Third, I had a husband who allowed me to be—yes, Gloria Steinem, allowed me! Given his traditional background and the time in which he grew up, this was pretty remarkable. He gave me permission to make good and bad decisions, work to exhaustion or exhilaration, and pull back or try something new.

This is not to say two ambitious people trying to carve out a life together didn't have some problems.

I was gone for weeks at a time, lecturing and doing television, leaving my husband in a house where the only forms of life were the leftovers growing in the refrigerator.

With the kids gone, we only had our jobs to talk about, which were at opposite poles. I talked about chatting with Lucille Ball and having dinner with Phyllis Diller. He talked about expelling a kid from school for wearing a T-shirt with an obscenity printed on it on the campus.

When we appeared together, there was unbelievable insensitivity from people who referred to him as Mr. Erma Bombeck, or worse, upon entering a room, someone would take my arm and he would be pushed aside to be swallowed up in the crowd.

For Better or for Work

And then there was my guilt.

I alone am responsible for refining guilt and elevating it to a sacrament.

"What kind of mother am I?" I whined to my best friend one day. "I don't even bake bread anymore."

She looked at me for a moment, then said, "You never baked bread."

"Oh God, I'm sorry for that too."

I was selfish. I wasn't being a good wife. My dish towels were gray and needed bleaching. The shelf paper hadn't been changed since 1960. I think I even assumed the blame for the Vietnam War.

My wardrobe expanded, my IRS returns increased, and my self-esteem grew before my eyes. Normally, this would have made Bill's world look smaller, but I discovered something about him I had not known when I married him.

Under that quiet, methodical, no-nonsense exterior beat the heart of a man who had a great sense of self. Men this secure are hard to come by. He had enjoyed his own rise to success and now sat back to enjoy mine. (I felt guilty about that too.) I hadn't been nearly as patient and supportive as he was when the tables were turned. When he was away from home a lot, I had nagged about being abandoned.

When he saw me taking myself too seriously, he would smile and say, "Hey Erma, I was at the library today and all of your books are . . . *in*."

I was always amazed that whenever I made a speech or personal appearance somewhere, someone would ask, "Isn't your husband with you?" My answer was always the same, "He doesn't come to work with me. I don't go to work with him."

It was a weird time between men and women. Our good friends were also a two-career family. She was one of the few women in a predominantly male profession. He accompanied her to a large convention where he found himself at a luncheon-style show for spouses with a perfume sample at his plate. When he found number 7 under his coffee cup, he discovered he had won the centerpiece. Later, the group was going shopping. He begged off, saying, "I have cramps."

Actually, Bill and I started to "protect" one another from the respective demands on our time. If his senior class was doing an original play, "Mary Ida Goes to Rio," he said, "I'll make an appearance for both of us." If I was judging a chili cookoff, I'd tell him, "Stay home. I got it covered." The only time he broke the rule was when he said he'd come

For Better or for Work

see me on *The Tonight Show*. He got lost in Burbank and didn't show up until the taping was over.

The two-paycheck family left a lot of marriages in its wake. One party pulled ahead too fast; the other too slow. One was stimulated; one was bored. One wanted to fly; the other one wanted to clip her wings.

How naive we had been. We had always thought if we got through the Hamburger Helper years, we were home free. Wrong. The times of struggle were a piece of cake compared to handling success. Everyone deals with it in his or her own way. There is no magic formula.

What it comes down to is what you need from one another. There was no reason for him to impress me. I already thought he was the smartest man I had ever met. Nor did I need him in the audience to laugh or to applaud me. He had done that for years.

What we needed from one another was normalcy, honesty, respect, and shared responsibility to keep it all in perspective. I watched a lot of marriages crumble in the '70s . . . mainly because the other half of the marriage was sitting home imagining all the glitz and glamour that followed the husband/wife who was out there dancing on table tops.

Erma Bombeck

What glamour? What glitz?

I endured drafty airplanes and beef tips that tasted like wing tips.

I slept in my underwear while my luggage slept in another city . . . ironed the next day's clothes on the toilet seat lid . . . autographed soggy cocktail napkins . . . stood at receptions for three hours listening to people tell me they write funny letters and are after my job.

I dealt with microphones that didn't work . . . 1 A.M. talk shows with people calling in who didn't even know who I was . . . TV make-up men who shaved my eyebrows, which never grew back again.

I sat three hours in a department store behind a stack of books, where the only exchange I had was with a woman who wanted directions to the rest room and a man who wanted to know the price of the desk.

And always there was the well-meaning welcoming committee who met you at the airport, followed you to the rest room, and insisted you see the Ohio River at 11 P.M.

The loneliness of being on the road is indescribable. You don't see anything (except the Ohio River in the dark). There are no "real" conversations. And frankly, you don't feel very productive. For this to have any meaning, just imagine a fifty-year-old woman sitting in a Houston hotel room at 10 A.M. on a Saturday morning watching cartoons for two hours before she's due to speak at a luncheon.

No one is more amazed that all of this worked than we are. We didn't sit down and analyze it, but maybe all of it came off because when the applause died down, when the people filed out of the auditorium and the lights went off . . . I had someone real to go home to.

Hi Mom! Hi Dad! I'm Home!

A commencement speaker at our younger son's graduation advised the class to "Go ye forth and multiply."

Not only did our kids not multiply . . . we couldn't even get them to go ye forth. I figured that when they were all twenty-something things they'd leave home and get on with their lives. Bill and I would feel alone, empty, and abandoned—for about fifteen minutes before we recovered.

Actually, they weren't out of the driveway before I had the rugs cleaned, the walls in their rooms stripped of posters, and nightly rental rates framed on the backs of the doors.

We were all set to be the self-centered, indulgent, materialistic adults God meant us to be. We ate better cuts of beef, went on vacations when we wanted, and brought the kids' bedrooms up to sanitary health standards and renamed them "guest rooms."

Then one day, the twenty-three-year-old popped into our kitchen with a sobering announcement. "I have found the perfect partner with whom I want to spend the rest of my life."

"Who is she?" I asked excitedly.

"She's in the driveway," he said. "Come meet her."

We rushed outside to see the future mother of our grandchildren. The object of his passion was a 1969 two-seater Karmann Ghia with a sticker still in the window that read $6,000.

"She's too good for you," I said flatly.

"I got it all figured out," he smiled. "I'll work two jobs and have two paychecks coming in."

"Are you sure you love it that much?"

"I've never been more sure of anything in my entire life," he said. "I'm sick of one-nighters that break down and repair bills that leave you feeling empty in the morning. You reach a point where you want someone to be there for you when you turn the key. Look at her, Mom. She's a classic."

I smiled weakly.

"Oh, by the way," he said, "I'm going to have to give up my apartment and move back home."

I told my feet to walk over and throw my arms around this large body. I told my mouth to say, "Welcome home, Son! We've missed you." But nothing moved. Bill and I just stood there. What was the matter with us? Aunt Em didn't act this way when Dorothy returned from Oz with that yapping dog, Toto. She was happy. Maybe it was the nagging feeling that all of us had changed.

Our friends said it might not be bad having an adult child live with us. He would keep us young. Besides, it might be stimulating to have a third party to talk with as an adult and share ideas. Not to mention bonding!

In your dreams. Grown children come home when they are out of work, out of sorts, out of money, or out of love.

There was a time when our California son (the first one to leave home) would call us with his flight number and arrival time. The whole family would swing into gear . . . Dad would gas up the car, I'd put a fresh flower in his old room, and the siblings would paint a sign, "Welcome Home," to hold up when he got off the plane.

After a half-dozen pickups, it got a little stale and we drew lots to see who had to pick him up. (His brother looked at his short stub once and announced, "If he has luggage, I'm leaving him there.") After about a year of popping in and out, we just slowed the car down and he hooked his arm onto the antenna and we dragged him home.

It wasn't that we didn't love seeing him; it's just that he was never there to see.

"Are you sure he's still home?" asked my husband.

"I think so. His clothes are still in the dryer and he's still getting phone calls." The kid was a blur the entire time he was there. So much for bonding.

In reality, we said good-bye to a child who ate baking soda and anything else in the refrigerator that didn't attack first. We said hello to an adult who complained that everything in the house had a stalk of wheat growing on the package.

He said good-bye to parents who enjoyed an active social life. He said hello to parents who got in their nightclothes right after dinner.

The child who had once set a record by running through a shower in less than thirty seconds now took an hour and thirty gallons of hot water to come clean.

The young parents who picked up toys and dirty socks now rebelled at returning his dinner plate to the kitchen.

A grown child who has come home to live can throw a marriage into a tailspin. Bill and I supported the wrong causes on our bumper stickers. We didn't take the world seriously enough. We watched mindless television and our friends were warmongers.

We dressed too young, thought too old, ate too fast, drove too slow. Our cars were too big. Our closets were too small. Home was not as he remembered it. Neither were the two people who lived there.

I walked into the kitchen one night to see our son standing in front of the refrigerator with both doors flung open and steam forming as the cold air clashed with the room temperature. He just stared.

"I don't suppose you could memorize the items until lunch, could you?"

"I don't know what I want," he mumbled. "I'm really hungry."

I slammed the door.

"Do we have any cold milk?"

Hi Mom! Hi Dad! I'm Home!

"Not anymore," I sighed.

He opened the doors again. "I need something . . ."

"How about a sweater?" I snapped, kicking the doors shut.

His being there was all Bill and I ever discussed. When he was home we worried he had no friends. When he was out, we worried what he was doing. When he had his own apartment, it was wonderful. We lived in ignorance. If he never called, we told ourselves he probably dropped a Bible on his foot and couldn't hobble to the phone. Under our roof, it was different. We felt compelled to outfit him with a beeper collar.

Somehow, both of us slipped back into the roles of parenting we thought we had left. Maybe God had given us a second chance to shape one up. His father nagged him about saving money. I got on his case about not cleaning his room. We gave opinions about his friends, his clothes, his life-style. We pursued the same theme . . . find a nice girl and settle down.

It was awkward being cast in our original roles in a revival of early family life. It was like trying to bring back the Mouseketeers and putting all of these middle-aged people in tap shoes and mouse ears. I was too old to lie awake and listen for the sound of the car to come home. I needed eighteen hours of sleep a night.

Bill and I had both grown territorial about our belongings, right down to which kitchen chairs we ate in and which ones we watched TV in. Life as we knew it would come to an end if the pencil became separated from the phone.

Sometimes I felt the arrangement was harder on the returning child than it was on us. He didn't know what role to play . . . the dependent child we wanted him to be or the independent man he aspired to be. So he did a little of both. When there were dishes to be done, he hid out in the bathroom like he did when he was nine. When it rained, he pulled his car into my spot in the garage and explained with authority, "You don't have a convertible with a torn top."

We lamely made up new rules daily, which we couldn't enforce. What were we going to do? Take away his bicycle privileges for a week?

One night he came into the kitchen and said, "Can we talk?" I poured him half a glass of milk and warned, "Don't spill it."

He took a deep breath and said, "I need to borrow some money to pay off the car so I can move into my own apartment."

Hi Mom! Hi Dad! I'm Home!

We had come full circle since that evening when Bill and I sat in my parents' kitchen begging for bucks for a bigger house. For the first time, I understood that the process of growing up has a predictable theme. All of our lives we try to please our parents. Our parents love us as long as we don't mess up, take their advice, are successful in their eyes, and when we are financially but not emotionally independent of them. It is a sad moment when you must admit to them that you're not ready to solo yet.

When he left, I reflected with some sadness on the parents he had remembered but who no longer existed. For a while, all of us thought we could recapture the rhythm, the easiness, the familiarity and humor that had made us a family. But we had all changed. We were worlds apart. Bill and I belonged to a generation of rules, tradition, and goals—a work ethic passed down to us by Depression parents.

He belonged to a group who traveled in packs, talked openly about their biological clocks, and listed, under "Occupation," "Finding myself." He had only to look in the dictionary under "yuppie" (young urban professional). His picture was there.

A House Morally Divided Cannot Stand One Another

❧

Rebellion in youth is a given. There has always been and always will be a generation gap between parents and their children. But this wasn't a mere gap with the Baby Boomers. This was a chasm that ran wide and deep.

Where our generation believed anything was possible, they believed nothing was possible. They had no desire to follow the paths laid by their parents that led to a college degree, a job, marriage, and babies. They created their own fashions, their own music, their own language, and their own timetables.

How did they expect us to get on with our lives until we had done our job . . . getting them saddled down with a thirty-year mortgage, a bad back, and a couple of kids to support?

The generation split was never more apparent than in the early '70s. I swung my car into the driveway one evening and came to a sudden stop. In my parking space was a pink van with purple scorpions painted all over its body. The bumper sticker read, IF YOU HAVEN'T SEEN GOD LATELY, GUESS WHO MOVED?

I had a strong feeling this vehicle did not belong to the pest control company.

I was right. Our kitchen looked like Woodstock. Young men with headbands wearing vests as shirts swilled cans of soft drinks. Young women dressed in bedspreads weighted by fringe swished around without makeup, their long hair cascading down their backs. They were "crashing" for a few days, visiting our daughter who was between jobs and had moved back home.

My house rules were simple. No drugs. No booze. And no one sleeps with a person of the opposite sex to whom he or she is not currently married.

Every time I delivered that announcement our daughter gave us that "can-you-believe-these-people—I-should-sell-tickets" look.

She wasn't fooling me. Every one of their parents lived where we lived . . . somewhere between Doris Day and Lawrence Welk. We weren't the ones changing the rules. They were.

I looked at my husband as he desperately tried to talk to a guy wearing an earring by asking, "How about those Cubs?" and wondered who are these people!

They didn't read. They didn't vote. They didn't save. They didn't cook. They didn't pursue a religion. They didn't even wear socks.

Later, as all three of our kids settled into their thirties without a mate, I took it personally. What were they waiting for? Did they look at us and see a couple who made marriage look like a sedative sold over the counter? Was it so boring they wanted no part of it?

Why were they so reluctant to make me a grandmother? Somewhere it is written that if a woman doesn't hold a baby in her arms every twenty years or so, she'll go crazy. Here I was fifty-one years old and all I had to show for it was a billfold with a couple of grandcats and granddogs.

What was I asking? Just twenty or thirty years of living on a shoestring so they could provide braces and tuition for their children . . . twenty or thirty lousy little years of worrying, counseling, advising, teaching, and being there.

A House Morally Divided Cannot Stand One Another

One evening, my daughter and I had possibly our two-hundredth conversation on the subject of marriage when she announced one of her friends was going to live with her significant other.

"Why don't they get married?" I asked.

"What difference does a piece of paper make?" she asked.

"Because marriage may be their last chance to grow up. It isn't dating anymore. It's the major league of relationships. Maybe the difference between relationships and being married is the former is a spectator sport and the latter is getting in the game and playing by all the rules."

"Right," she said, "and suppose it doesn't work."

"If you want guarantees, go live with a Sears battery," I said.

My words fell on pierced ears covered with thirty pounds of hair. "Is this because you talked to Marianna today and she told you about her new grandchild?"

"The kid is three months old, has a ninety-word vocabulary, is toilet trained, and can work the microwave," I said sadly.

"Be patient, Mom. We're in no hurry. You'll be a grandmother someday."

"If it doesn't happen soon," I said, "my

grandchild and I will be in diapers together."

As the value placed on marriage diminished, new rules of morality took precedence. Cohabitation, as I understood it, was a honeymoon without a marriage. Sometimes they called them "relationships." We heard the words "casual sex" a lot. I asked my son about it one night when he dropped by.

"You're wasting your time," yawned my husband.

"Mom, it's when a person has a relationship with someone who attracts them."

"You mean it's real laid-back?"

"I'll pretend you didn't say that," he said. "It's like an encounter that is going nowhere . . . something impersonal, a fling with someone they barely know and will never see again."

"You're saying they don't know their names?"

"Of course they know their names," he said.

"Then how come Willie Kennedy Smith was called Mike by his rape accuser and he called her Cathie, which wasn't her real name either?"

"Okay, so they don't always know their names."

"So you are telling me that kids know the

name of U2's drummer and they don't know the names of people they're sleeping with?"

"Make your point, Mom."

"The point is, you register at weddings to tell people you were there. You have business cards printed to introduce yourself. You wouldn't be caught dead at a reunion without a name tag. Wouldn't you think a sex partner could at least sign the guest book?"

He shook his head. "You still don't get it."

"Sure I do. Casual sex is mostly made for TV. It's an impersonal, anonymous union between two bored adults. No reservations needed. Dress down."

Bill had a better handle on what this generation was about than I did. Mother's Day was over and I didn't want to admit it.

"Let it go," he said. "We're getting three adults with ideas, humor, creativity, who are putting together their own lives. Isn't that what we taught them to do?"

It had happened so slowly, I barely noticed it. But the signs were there that my power and influence had diminished.

It was time to get on with our own marriage.

But one day a miracle happened. One of my daughter's friends, Dawn, announced she was getting married.

At last, someone was turning to tradition.

I hugged Dawn and said, "You must tell me what you need so I'll know what to get for a wedding present."

"I'm registered at Bullock's' bridal registry," she said.

My arms dropped to my side. Here was a young woman I had never seen in anything but bib overalls and Birkenstocks. She had lived on beaches for six years, eating seaweed and raw berries and playing the guitar. The closest she had ever come to domesticity was a plastic fork from McDonald's tucked in her sweatband. She had re-entered civilization and her first words were "bridal registry."

At Bullock's my daughter and I pored over her selections. "Look at this," I said, "Wallace, Wedgwood, and Waterford. Where do kids learn words like that? They certainly don't pick them up from their parents."

"We have to make a decision," she said dryly. "How about we both go together and buy a pickle fork in her pattern."

"Is she the one who danced naked on a car hood at a Grateful Dead concert?"

"Yes. Do we spring for the pickle fork? It's $48."

"It's perfect," I said.

I dreaded the idea of attending Dawn's bridal shower. I hadn't been to one since we sat around making little brides out of crepe paper and clothespins and drinking sweet punch that made your face break out.

Dawn's shower was different. She unwrapped gifts of condoms and lingerie. Halfway through the evening, a male stripper danced around wearing a string and a pouch and guests put dollar bills wherever they dared.

If I thought tradition was making a comeback, I was wrong. Dawn was married in a meadow just off the highway. Both read a passage from *Catcher in the Rye,* and a minister from the Church of What's Happening officiated. Her husband thanked us for the "lock picker."

It was a strange time to be traditional people in a traditional marriage. Our expectations were at opposite ends of the spectrum.

We must have seemed like aliens to them. Whatever it was, for a ten-year period they were in and out of our house with their crates of records and CDs, their stereos and speakers, an assortment of pets, friends, dirty laundry, and rusted cars.

My husband bought a T-shirt that read, HOW CAN I SAY GOOD-BYE WHEN YOU WON'T LEAVE?

They didn't laugh a lot either.

1979

Run for Your Life

❧❀❧

It was cold in Boston. I could feel it through my raincoat and see it on the breaths of 7,877 men and women in shorts and bare arms at the starting line of the Boston Marathon.

As I tried to make a path for myself through the spectators to get a better view, I felt like a pinball bouncing against one obstacle after another. Who were these people who looked like they had just survived a death march? My body collided with a bony woman in a ponytail. I had cooked bigger turkeys than her. Why would anyone in their right mind want to run 26 miles and 385 yards in the rain just to end up in a parking garage on a cot with stomach cramps and blisters on their feet?

Why would my husband want to be one of them? At fifty-two, he had decided he wanted to devote his life to pain. It was the first time in our marriage we had a conflict we couldn't resolve. He had jogged before, but it had gotten out of hand. I told him he was obsessed with running. He said what he did with his time shouldn't bother me. The truth is I was jealous of his infatuation with it, ticked off with his discipline, and alienated by something I was too lazy to share.

I never thought we'd go through life like matched luggage. The only thing I had ever hoped for was that we would hate the same people together, be angry at our children at the same time, and deteriorate at the same pace. The problem was . . . I was beginning to look like a first wife.

The obsession with youth seemed to have touched everyone but me. There were more cosmetic surgeons listed in the yellow pages than there were plumbers. People didn't eat anymore. They grazed. (My parents were buying oat laxatives.) Exercise had become a major religion.

What I saw in the mirror each morning

was not a pretty sight. The 113-pound bride now weighed 148 pounds. How much longer could I go on telling people I sagged because I carried the baby low . . . when the baby was twenty-one years old now? How long would it be before Bill wouldn't turn on a light in the bedroom for fear of losing his sight by catching a glimpse of me?

I didn't do anything to my hair, and gray strands were beginning to zing out of nowhere. My upper arms could have supported a torch in New York Harbor.

All I would have needed was for Bill to look at me and say, "My God, Erma, your rear looks like a Mayflower van."

It would hurt. I'd cry a little. Go to my room. Maybe slam a door or two. Call a good lawyer to arrange a separation. But at least it would motivate me to lose a few pounds.

But did he do that? Oh no, he said things like "Can I get you anything while I'm up?"

What did he expect me to say, "Sure, two chairs in front of the refrigerator"?

Without even realizing it, I was jealous of his new health kick and the time he devoted to it. It was probably the first major split of interest we had had where I was neither understanding, appreciative, nor supportive of what he was doing.

Erma Bombeck

Every time he said, "No pain—no gain," I wanted to slap him. I came from stock who believed in miracles.

One of my aunts bought a mail-order jumpsuit made out of parachute silk with a nozzle attachment. She was supposed to lose weight if she attached the nozzle to her vacuum sweeper and turned on the switch. The hot stale air would fill the garment until she looked like the Goodyear blimp. This would either burn off the fat or blow it into the atmosphere. No one was really sure of the dynamics. I'll never forget the sight of her hovering near the ceiling if I live to be a hundred.

Secretly, I tried to shape up. I did one diet where you ate one kind of fruit for two full days, then changed fruits for the next two. I bought jars of mud from the Dead Sea that was supposed to take the tire marks out of my skin. I had my body pounded, slapped, steamed, baked, kneaded, iced, basted, and greased.

But running for ten miles every day? Please. He would jog into the kitchen after a run with a towel around his neck. "Look at the time," he bragged, "and I'm not even breathing heavily."

"Don't give me that!" I said sarcastically. "You just sucked up the newspaper through your nose."

Run for Your Life

"You know," he panted, "maybe you should try jogging. It firms up the muscles, gets you going in the mornings, and besides, it gives you discipline."

"So does a war," I said, "and I'm not going there either."

The age gap between us began to widen. The thinner he got, the more I ate. The more energy he had, the tireder I got. We seemed to be living two different lives.

My vanity had never gotten beyond the main aisle of the cosmetic departments where they had skin specialists ready to assist you.

"You need a repair kit," one of them said one day.

"Are we talking extra parts?" I asked.

"No, no," she said, "it's just that there is a cell breakdown and you need toning and firming, especially around your eyes. Just something to take away those laugh lines."

Laugh lines! Was she crazy? Here I was trapped in a time warp of fifty-somethings who all had aging pictures in the attic while I looked like Manuel Noriega with a bad permanent. What did I have to laugh about?

I was entering an era where, not too far down the road, women would pull into a gas station, roll down the car windows, and say,

"Let fifteen pounds of air out of the cheeks, pump another thirty pounds in the lips and chest, wax the mustache, and oh . . . put a patch on the left rear buttock. If you have any bargains on liver spot removal or super savers on crow's feet, tell me now."

Already, a doctor in Chicago was talking about reversing the aging process. The kicker is that it only had an impact on the way your body looked. It had no effect on failing eyes and dying brain cells. In other words, you could look youthful on the outside, but inside you would still be growing old.

What would it profit you to look like Arnold Schwarzenegger on the beach if you could never put down your towel farther than two feet from a rest room?

Three hours and twenty-two minutes into the Boston Marathon, Bill ran across the finish line. He had done something remarkable.

I had to question myself—Why I had been so jealous. Was I threatened? Was I intimidated? Was I on a guilt trip?

Probably all of the above. What did I expect from a marriage? Did I want to be like a couple I saw in Hawaii wearing matching shirts? Or the woman who was so dependent

on her husband he walked her to the restroom door—and waited for her. Or, God forbid, the woman whose husband never retired
without her and stood at the door whining,
"You coming to bed now?"

What made the marriage interesting were
the things we didn't have in common.

At the hotel as he showered, I yelled at
him through the door, "You ready to pack
some carbohydrates?"

"Sure. Where's a good Italian restaurant?"

"Follow me. You're on my turf now."

Marriage. A blending of talents.

Change Roles ... and Dance as Fast as You Can

❧❧

I kicked my luggage into the darkened hallway and followed a beacon of light that came from the family room.

I had been on the road for ten days doing *Good Morning America* pieces. There were deadlines facing me for the column and three days of stumping for the ERA in Missouri, and the family was having Thanksgiving dinner at my house.

On the screen was a perky woman with blonde silky hair making homemade gingerbread cookies brushed with softly beaten egg whites and then painted with gold leaf. Her name was Martha Stewart, and I felt like Elvis

Presley when he saw Robert Goulet on the screen. I wanted to get a gun, shoot the screen, and make her fade to black.

Bill was mesmerized as he watched her go to the smoke pit in her backyard and check on her turkey. She returned and smiled warmly at the camera as she filled a hollowed-out pumpkin to hold the soup course. She announced she was going to give us her recipe for cassoulet.

"Hi, Honey," said my husband, not taking his eyes off the screen. "You got a pencil and something to write on? Take this down."

Erma, the idiot, dug in the handbag and emerged with a ballpoint and a blank check and started to write while Martha dictated: six five-pound ducks, two cups of fresh duck fat, sixteen pounds of Great Northern beans, and six pounds of garlic sausage."

"Are you crazy?" I said tiredly, throwing down the pen.

"Shhh. There are more ingredients."

Actually, there were twenty-two ingredients in all . . . enough to feed everyone attending the Super Bowl or six sumo wrestlers.

Exhausted, I stared into space. I was a woman who had it all, and if I had any more I'd be in intensive care. Bill was sitting there in a robe and fuzzy slippers munching pop-

Erma Bombeck

corn. I used to do that. It was he who used to come home late and beat. We had changed roles without even noticing.

"The porch light is out," I said.

"I bought new bulbs," he said. "Maybe you can change it on the weekend."

"What's new with the kids?"

"I went to a basketball game Monday with Andy. He's good. The others checked in. There's cold meat loaf in the refrigerator. I didn't know if your plane would be late. You can heat it up if you want."

"I need a pair of your underwear to auction off at an ERA rally next Tuesday."

"Do I have to be in them?"

"No."

"Then help yourself."

Trading roles wasn't something a lot of men talked about. It was a macho thing. But secretly, the ones who did it seemed to enjoy it. After years of racing with the rats it was a good life. They enjoyed being autonomous, setting their own schedules, and working under less stress. He could look back on a successful career and had nothing to prove.

For women like me, who loved the adventure of going beyond the driveway and filching little bottles of shampoo and bath gel from hotels, it was a marriage made in heaven.

Change Roles . . . and Dance as Fast as You Can

I drifted back to Martha, who was gathering Tellicherry peppercorns, orrisroot powder, bayberry bark, senna pods, lemon verbena, and rosehips from her backyard for potpourri. I had no idea what she just said.

"Is it all right if I watch the news?" I asked.

"This will be over in a minute," he said.

In all honesty, men changed a few rules when they became what was referred to as househusbands. Bill didn't make beds, cook, dust, do laundry, windows or floors, or give birth. What he did do was pay bills, call people to fix the plumbing, handle investments and taxes, volunteer big time, take papers to the garage, change license plates, get the cars serviced, and pick up the cleaning. If women had had that kind of schedule, who knows, we'd probably still be in the home.

It was as if they wanted to show us how easy it all was. Try it with hot flashes and then tell me what a religious experience it is.

Because he was basically cheap, he would never start the dishwasher until every dish in the house was dirty. Sofa cushions would be removed only if there was a promise of money under them.

You could have measured time by the dust on the coffee table, but the knives in the kitchen were sharp enough to cut through a bank safe.

He was impatient with housework. The refrigerator was never cold enough, the water heater never hot enough, the lights never bright enough, the drains never large enough, and the coffeemaker never fast enough. It's the way men are. I had a brother-in-law who made one of those ducks with the wings that spin around when the wind blows for his backyard. He was always tinkering with it. It never flew fast enough.

Bill's car became a Meals on Wheels, and our dish pattern was white plastic foam. Our homemaking styles were different. Whenever he picked up a pizza, he took along a beach towel to wrap it in so it would remain hot. I would never have done that.

Slowly and insidiously, order began creeping into our lives . . . we had never had that under my reign. He kept a diary of the day's events: how far he had run and in how many minutes . . . who called (even if it was a wrong number) . . . and what he did that day. Every Christmas, he dredged up statistics from the diary—the height of the Christmas tree we had bought the year before, what kind it was, and how much it cost. No one cared.

Change Roles . . . and Dance as Fast as You Can

He had a thing about manuals. If someone were to rob the house and succeeded in stealing our manual on the microwave or the disposer, we had an extra copy of it hidden in a filing cabinet in the hallway. I was to sleep better at night knowing this. He was a methodical man who ran the house like the Pentagon. One day I had started to open the refrigerator door when I noticed a white piece of lined paper flapping from it with two columns marked IN and OUT.

"What is this?" I asked.

"Isn't that great?" he said proudly. "It's a record of what is in the refrigerator and what is taken out so you don't have to stand there with the door open. I got the idea from our safe-deposit box. When we take a document out of the box, I record it on a piece of paper . . . or when I return our passports, I record that too."

"They're going to put you in a home," I said.

"It works," he said excitedly. "Look here, the cabbage roll had seven ins and seven outs, signifying no one knew what it was until he bit into it."

I put on my glasses and noted baking soda was marked in and out and in again with a notation, "Needs work."

Erma Bombeck

Sometimes I went grocery shopping with Bill, which was a big mistake. I'd throw a box of cookies into the cart and he would take them out and ask, "Did you mean to buy thirteen ounces for the same price as a pound of the same cookies?"

Or he'd pick up a quart of milk out of the cart and say, "Is it important that the expiration date was two days ago, or do you have a recipe calling for sour milk?"

Because of his health kick, he had turned my kitchen into a field of oats and grain. We had oat brownies, oat breads, oat cereals, oat pretzels, oat muffins, and oat waffles. I picked up a hot dog bun that looked like it had dropped on the floor. It was made of oats.

I complained, but to no avail. "Oats are good for you," he insisted.

"If they're so good for you then how come we owned a horse once who wouldn't eat them unless they were coated with molasses?"

Ironically, none of this bothered me. You survive being isolated any way you can. I had been there. With me, I had crocheted fifteen pairs of bedroom slippers one year for Christmas and took a cake decorating course at the Y. With him, he had lunch once a month with the guys and installed a microchip under the toilet seat that played "Lara's Theme" from *Dr. Zhivago.*

My life in the fast lane didn't bother him. He had been there. He seemed to know that, in time, spending five hours waiting for a plane to be fixed in Atlanta would grow stale and that when there were no more mountains to climb, your thoughts would turn to home. It was just my turn.

There was a lot of press given to the Phil Donahues and Alan Aldas, who epitomized the men who understood women. But for every one of them, there were hundreds of men who also "got it," keeping pace with a changing society. I was married to one of them. He listened to my anger over the inequities of being female. He acknowledged I had something to give beyond a decent pot roast. He discovered long ago that a marriage dominated by one partner wasn't much of a marriage.

Our marriage had been like a relay race. He had run around the track and handed the torch to me while I took my lap. But it took both of us to finish the race.

Not a lot of people understood this relationship. Our kids couldn't explain how it worked. Neither could most of our friends. Role reversal was foreign to my parents.

Erma Bombeck

We took vacations together and we took them separately. The latter gave many people pause, but it all came down to trust. We never worried about one another. I was too tired for an affair and he needed me to send out the Christmas cards, so we were pretty secure.

His idea of paradise was fishing. (Remember, I got the fishing license for our first anniversary?) I hated the smell of it . . . and the boredom of it . . . and, in fact, I hated anything that was situated more than a mile from a mall.

When he wasn't on a trip with the guys, he was watching the fishing shows on television every Saturday morning. He'd appear at the breakfast table dressed in jeans and a flannel shirt, with the first two buttons open, over a turtleneck sweater. Then he'd place himself squarely in front of the TV set to watch Bubba and Roy (they were always Bubba and Roy) from Arkansas or Oklahoma. Bubba and Roy looked like good old country boys, but they had a boat and rods and reels that cost more than our first house.

They also talked funny. Bubba would say, "I have a feeling you're gonna need more than that eighty-pound test line, Roy," or Roy would break the silence with, "I'll tell you the truth, Bubba, I never kissed a fish with bad breath." They stood up in the boat all the time, never wore life vests, and the most amazing thing is every time they cast out their lines, they got a strike. They never caught anything small or humiliating.

Me? I liked to go, with my friends, to spas where I could dress up in cute little outfits with matching headbands, drink herbal tea, and touch my ear to my left knee in time with Neil Diamond. (No matter where I am today, when I hear the theme from *Exodus,* I squeeze my buttocks together.)

I'd lose two pounds in a week, come home, have a glass of water, and be right back up where I was before I left home, but it was good to get away from the deadlines.

It was good to see the gender barriers come tumbling down. Maybe if more married couples would trade jobs, there would be more of an appreciation for what each partner does or doesn't do.

Maybe we would not have had husbands who came home and asked their wives, "What kind of a day did you have?" and left the room while their wives were answering the question.

Maybe we would have had wives who would have welcomed a husband who had worked late with a better greeting than, "Michael needs braces and we're being audited."

I looked at Bill staring intently at the TV screen as Martha Stewart checked her roasting pig in a pit in her backyard like he was watching a documentary.

I fell asleep in the chair.

We had come full circle.

Technology's Coming! Technology's Coming!

❧❀❧

Bill and I stood patiently outside the door of our friends Sandy and Ben's house as their doorbell played "Fly Me to the Moon." Every time we visited them it was like waiting in a line for Disneyland's Tomorrowland. They were technology junkies. Their lives were dominated by every new product that came down the pike.

They bought cordless phones that measured their cardiovascular workouts, radar detectors for their cars, and electric alarm systems for their attaché cases. Their garage held two cars that had better vocabularies than Sandy.

Erma Bombeck

They owned a digital alarm clock with a built-in flashlight and his and her alarms. They bought an electronic mail detector so they didn't have to make all those long trips to the mailbox (which was a slot in their front door).

The door opened and Ben grabbed us by the shoulders and pulled us in. "You gotta see this," he said excitedly, dragging us into the kitchen. "Sandy!" he shouted, "do the stove for them." On cue, Sandy walked like a robot to the sink and filled a saucepan with water. From there she went to the stove and without so much as touching a button set the pan on the smooth surface. It began to boil immediately. She then removed the pan and placed her hand on the spot where the pan had been. She smiled triumphantly.

"Do you always have to put your hand on the stove after you've cooked something?" asked Bill.

"No, no," said Ben, "you missed the point. You could if you wanted to. The cooking unit is programmed only to cook. Pretty amazing, huh? How about a drink?"

As Ben plugged in his electric cocktail stirrer, I glanced around Sandy's kitchen, which she called a food center. There was a computerized bread baker, thermometer spoon, trash compactor, electric knife sharpener, salad spinner, and SaladShooter. Sandy and Ben had embraced the '80s and all of its technology. Bill and I just hung back like it was a blind date. The only concession we had made to automation was a smoke alarm. It told me when our dinner was ready.

No one came right out and said so, but technology put stress on marriages and relationships. It was fine when the devices worked, but when they didn't we tended to take our frustrations out on one another. In some cases, they were a catalyst for violence.

Neither Bill nor I was what you would call technology-friendly. I couldn't fold a box at Christmas without therapy. There was no doubt in our minds that half of the people in the Betty Ford clinic were there because they tried to program their VCRs. But we were caught in a decade of change that proved to be more than we could handle.

Then one morning, on schedule, Bill pulled out a two-quart saucepan, put a half cup of skim milk in it, and set it on the stove to warm for his coffee. As usual, he forgot about it, and it boiled over onto the stove.

"Remember what we said about mainstreaming into the '80s?" he said, grabbing a roll of paper towels to wipe up the mess.

"What are you saying?" I asked.

"I'm saying we probably should break down and buy a microwave oven."

"Let me get this straight. You want to buy a seven-hundred-watt oven with five pages of precautions and twenty-seven pages of operation instructions because of a little spilled milk?"

"Sandy and Ben swear by theirs."

"Sandy uses hers to store her cookbooks."

We argued. I lost. The microwave came to live in our kitchen. The book of instructions could have made a twelve-hour miniseries. "Guess how many men it takes to replace a lightbulb in your microwave?" I asked, leafing through the manual.

When he didn't answer I said, "Four. Two nuclear physicists, one man with asbestos hands, and an authorized service representative who determines the bulb's availability.

"Hey," I said sarcastically, "here's a whole chapter on probe cooking. When was the last time you had probe?"

"Lighten up," he commanded. "You act like we've just bought two tickets for a space shuttle. It's only an oven, for crying out loud. Why are you opposed to something that is going to save you time?"

Time is the key word here. I kept a log of the time saved. It was underwhelming.

Technology's Coming! Technology's Coming!

Time to read the manual: 20 minutes.

Time arguing about whether my good china goes in an atmosphere that could explode eggs: 10 minutes.

Heating time for a half cup of milk: 30 seconds.

Time to treat finger for burns when I stuck it in the milk to see whether it was hot enough: 5 minutes.

Time to heat the coffee, which had turned cold while we messed around heating the milk: 1 minute.

Technology has never been singled out as one of the major causes of domestic unrest, but it is.

For me, the microwave was a test. If we could survive it, the gates would open to all the gadgetmeisters had to offer. We'd eventually turn into Ben and Sandy, surrounded by our new toys.

From then on, there wasn't a day we didn't challenge our marriage. We unpacked the VCR. That's as far as we got. For weeks, we circled it and promised ourselves we'd let it work its magic.

Mentally, I had begun to think of other uses for it. Maybe we could put legs on it and use it for an end table or release the ejection slot and put a plant in it.

Erma Bombeck

Then one Friday when we decided to go out to dinner, Bill suggested we tape "Dallas." He picked up the instruction manual and began to read. In a burst of sentiment, I wanted to be near him. I put my hand over his and said, "I want you to know that whatever happens, I think you're the bravest man I have ever met."

He jerked away. "Good Lord, we're making too much of this. We're not dismantling a bomb. It's only a harmless VCR. You read and I'll push the buttons."

"You want me to read the pages on how to use the manual?"

"Skip all of that," he said, "and get on with how to record a show when we're not here."

I traced the words slowly with my fingers and read them aloud. "You have to swing down the cover of the programming button compartment at the right of the clock and set speed switch to LP, SP, or SLP before you insert the cassette."

"The clock is blinking," he said excitedly.

"Then you screwed up. You have to go back and reprogram that particular memory position."

"How do I do that?"

"Press the daily button. Not the 2-W, you ninny, or you're back to square one."

Technology's Coming! Technology's Coming!

"I think I've got A.M.," he said.

"Well, you want P.M. You should be able to select one of the eight programs by pressing the button with the number and the minutes and the hours. Do you see the days of the week flashing?"

"Everything is flashing."

"Don't forget to press the record-stop time. Are the letters CH flashing? If so, you're ready for the channel selector switch. Hey, I think you've got something. I see Miss Ellie and J.R. You're recording! You've done it."

"It is not recording. I have done nothing," he said slowly. "You are seeing the actual program on the set. We might just as well sit down and watch it."

It was a bitter pill to swallow. The machine was smarter and stronger than we were. It was only a preview of things to come.

Technology would affect the way we lived, communicated, ate, voted, raised our children, worked, shopped, traveled, and dealt with problems.

In an age when we should have settled into a comfortable and familiar rut, Bill locked himself in the bathroom for three days trying to set a runner's watch. I hurt myself kicking a talking scale that said, "Remove fillings in your teeth, Bimbo." Our cameras were obsolete before we could get film in them. Our clocks blinked; our friends beeped. Cellular phones were everywhere and pulled short of phone implants. Our children couldn't write without a computer and automatic speller, and people faxed out for their lunch.

Our kids were thoroughly disgusted with us. As they watched us stumbling around pushing buttons and twirling dials, we not only lost face, our IQs plummeted to single digits.

"Why don't you get an answering device on your phone?" one of our sons nagged.

"Why? Why do we need a recording to tell someone we're out? If no one answers, we're not there. That's not too hard to figure."

Change in a marriage is always difficult. Not only with the principles, but those that evolve in the world around you. It seemed as if we had become obsolete overnight. We couldn't get film for our cameras, buy carbon paper for the office, eight-track cassettes for an old stereo at the cabin, or parts for my typewriter.

Our only choice was to join the majority.

One day I got into my car, which nagged me about my emergency brake being on, my door being open, and my seat belt not being fastened. I went to the bank, which was an automatic teller, used an elevator with an automatic voice, ordered lunch by yelling into a small box with a recording inside and saw only a hand when I claimed my bag, made reservations at a restaurant for dinner on a recording that asked me to leave what time and how many in my party, and called our three children who were out right now but if I left my message would get back to me.

I had functioned all day long without hearing a human voice.

The television set that in our early married years had occupied a spot the size of a coaster now covered an entire wall and was like a magnet. We were drawn to it every night after dinner. When the electricity went off in the house, we didn't mind that we couldn't use the stove or keep our drinks cold. It didn't matter that the garage door wouldn't go up or that we were thrown into darkness. Who cared if the heat or air conditioner went off. If we couldn't watch TV, there was no reason to go on living. It was one of the few things we shared and were able to operate until a bit of technology came upon the scene: a remote TV tuner.

There was nothing egalitarian about the TV tuner. Every night after dinner there was a scramble for it. My husband, Darth Vader, regarded it as his personal "force" of good over evil.

I'd be sitting there watching *Dallas* and just after Sue Ellen would say, "Miss Ellie, I've got to sort things out. I thought I'd go to—" a ninety-pound walrus would flash on the screen and Bill Conrad's voice would say, ". . . the Bering Sea with thousands of other bulls to mate."

Once again he had changed the channel without asking me. I knew in my heart as long as he held that little box, I'd never get back to Southfork.

Bill never saw a TV commercial. It was like one subliminal experience after another as denture creams, breakfast cereals, and wine coolers all ran together.

Sometimes he hid the tuner from me, but I knew he had it when I was watching Liv Ullmann in a deep-meaning film and she turned into a pizza commercial that turned into Frank Gifford who turned into the Boston Pops who turned into two sumo wrestlers.

The conversion to Technology Я Us was so slow, we didn't realize what we had become until one Saturday we opened the front door to greet two guests. We knew they were coming because all the outdoor lights went on automatically when a car broke the beam at the end of the driveway.

It was Ben and Bernice. (He divorced Sandy when she ran off with a compact home shredder salesman.)

"Nice lights," said Ben, "but they're obsolete. I just got a doorbell intercom security system . . . just so you know who's on the other side of the door. Did you ever figure out how to set your runner's watch?"

Bill held out his arm proudly in answer.

"Get rid of it," said Ben, "and invest in one of the newer models. It takes your blood pressure at the same time."

Bill steered him toward the kitchen and said proudly, "Erma, do the cookbook."

I sat down on a stool in front of my personal computer and punched up menu suggestions, family allergies to certain foods, the contents of my pantry, and copies of my favorite recipes.

Ben and Bernice exchanged smiles. "I used to use the computer for all that. Now I have a laminizer for all my recipes," said Bernice. "It's so easy. A real time saver. My God, Ben, these people still dial their own phones."

When they left, I walked down the hall-way with sonic bug killers in the sockets, flipped off the VCR, which had been recording a show while we ate dinner, unplugged the towel warmer, and pressed a lever with my foot to lower the toilet seat lid.

I felt like a 33 1/3 record. I still had a lot of music in me . . . but there was no place to play it.

1981

The Separation

I was always intrigued by what I called the Velcro Couples. They were marrieds who were joined at the hip. Whenever they entered a room together, they were always holding hands. When she sneezed, he got a cold. She called him every morning to see if he got to work safely. When he talked she gazed into his eyes, and every time he told the same stupid joke about the priest, the rabbi, and the minister, she'd fall off her chair with laughter.

Bill and I had a marriage so flexible that

whenever we went on vacation together, someone would invariably ask me how long I had been widowed.

We were two independent people who happened to be married to one another.

In 1981, a contract with ABC gave me the option of developing a sitcom for television. The odds of creating, writing, and having a series picked up and aired on the first try were about the same as a terrorist hijacking a plane to Richmond, Indiana. Bill and I talked about it and he said, "Go for it."

I pitched an idea, the network liked it, we made it into a pilot, and miracle of all miracles, *Maggie* was put on the fall schedule. When I heard the news I felt like Robert Redford in *The Candidate,* who, when he was finally elected to office, said, "What do I do now?"

It obviously wasn't a job I could phone in from my kitchen in Arizona, so the first step was for me to find an apartment in L.A. I could fly home every Friday night and fly back every Monday morning.

It marked the first time in thirty-two years we had lived apart.

For many women, driving in a city the size of Los Angeles would have been intimidating. I actually fell into a pattern. I rented a car at LAX every Monday, got on the freeway, forgot to exit, and ended up staring at the Pacific Ocean in Santa Monica. I stopped at a service station for directions on how to get to Beverly Hills. In four months, I never deviated once from this route.

I worked five days a week from six in the morning to eight at night, lived on a diet of burnt popcorn and diet colas, and pretended to know what I was doing.

I had the social life of a leper. At a time of my life when I should have been having coffee in the morning and popping estrogen, I was loading up scripts with two "damns" and one "hell" to trade the censors for a toilet-training joke.

My parking space had my name inscribed in chalk. In my insecurity, I looked daily for a man with a garden hose.

As an executive producer of a series, I was required to be insurable. A doctor dropped by my office one morning and asked, "How do you feel?" "Fine," I said. "A little hypertension."

"I didn't hear that," he smiled, making a notation. Then he said, "Let me take your temperature."

I waited for him to take a thermometer out of his pocket. Instead, he walked around the desk and put his cheek next to mine and said "98.6."

Erma Bombeck

I showed him to the door.

As I was telling this bizarre story to the receptionist, he poked his head in the door and added, "I meant to tell you, I have my SAG (Screen Actors' Guild) card. If you ever need a doctor in your series, I'm available."

I was living out every married woman's fantasy. High-powered job, alone in a big city, and a steady date at home every Saturday night. I could eat onion sandwiches, go to bed when I pleased, and did not have to cook if I didn't feel like it.

But I discovered something about marriage I hadn't appreciated before. Life isn't much when you no longer have anyone to think about except yourself. I had always fed off of everyone else's problems. It justified my own existence. Now, everything I did was for myself.

What did I have left? Shopping in overnight supermarkets . . . holding a wake if a plant in my rented apartment died . . . and rejoicing in my weekly view of the Pacific Ocean at Santa Monica.

I had never appreciated before the luxury of having someone to share my life with. Without my husband, I felt ordinary. As a couple, there wasn't anything I wouldn't consider.

The Separation

What made all of it bearable was I have never worked with such a group of dedicated, professional people in all my life. They were great! But they had homes to go to every night and people to share their day with. I had a lot of time to think, and although it's not much of a revelation, I discovered work is not enough. It is no substitute for someone to laugh with, cry with, or worry with.

After six episodes of *Maggie* I saw the man with the garden hose come into the parking lot one day and wash away the name on my parking spot. The show was canceled. Hollywood has a bizarre way of telling you. Dinah Shore once said she knew her show was canceled when Euell Gibbons (a naturalist who used to eat plants and tree bark from the forest) ate her desk.

I had mixed feelings. On one hand, I felt I had let thirty people down. They were without jobs. On the other hand, it meant I could go home and pick up my life.

There was the furniture to ship home, the apartment to vacate, the rental car to turn in, and the good-byes. Aaron Priest, my agent, was the first to appear. As I was on the set trying to figure out what to tackle first, a second figure appeared on the sound stage. Bill had taken the first plane out of Phoenix to help me clean up.

Erma Bombeck

If this had been a movie, he would have said, "I told you so. You were just out of your element."

That didn't happen. He had allowed me to pursue this venture without guilt and either soar or fall on my face.

Together, we scrubbed the small kitchen floor of the apartment before taking leave.

As we locked up and prepared to leave the complex, Bill said, "I don't know how you did it . . . moving to a big city, meeting new people, doing a job you have never done before . . . alone. That's the sign of a successful woman. Tell you what, before we fly home, let's take a drive out to the ocean at Santa Monica. Which way do I go?"

My eyes darted around nervously. "From here?"

"Yeah, why?"

"Because the only way I can get there is from the airport. That's where I make my wrong turn."

It would have been such a poignant ending to a chapter on separation, but no, he had to see the lousy ocean!

Unsafe over 55

❧

Marriage in our fifties can be described with one word: frenetic. Panic set in. There was a scramble to place our bets before the window closed . . . fill up the car with gas before the freeway . . . dance the last dance before the orchestra went home.

We stuffed our bodies into little convertibles built for trolls. I wore sunglasses that covered half my face. Bill took a seminar in photography and a course in fly casting. I took a class in Oriental cooking.

We binged on traveling. Both of us threw up on cruise ships, fell off of camels, and explored bat caves. We were the oldest couple on a white-water rafting expedition in

Costa Rica. If we could drink the water and didn't have to take shots, we didn't want to go there.

We were like two crazy people rushing for the last lifeboat on the *Titanic*. It wasn't a restlessness. It was the realization that we had lived half a century. Your vision of the future gets a little out of focus at this age.

One day, in my euphoria to fill in every space of our dance program, I said to Bill, "I got it! Why don't we build the house of our dreams?"

When he tells the story of my proposal to people he says I had that same look on my face as Mickey Rooney when he took Judy Garland by the shoulders and screamed, "I got it! We'll put on a Broadway show! In the barn!"

I don't know why I said it. We were two people who couldn't wait for a traffic light to turn green, let alone build a house together.

He cautioned, "Think about it. Remember when we moved into this house and every time we flushed, steam would pour out of the bowl because the plumber had hooked it up wrong?"

I nodded my head slowly.

"And what about the time we moved and they gave us that little booklet about planning ahead? And the moving van couldn't fit on the footbridge and we had to transport ten rooms of furniture by dolly?"

"Yes, but—"

"And surely you haven't forgotten about Mr. Sluggard and Curly, Larry, and Moe?"

"It won't be like that," I said. "This is different. This is a house we are going to create together like a baby. Look upon it as a new offspring carrying the fruits of my creativity and your financial assistance. We will both conceive it, carry it, and be there at its birth."

I have never heard so much screaming at a conception before. We argued over tiles, paint, spigots, water heater, trash compactors, doors, hardware, light fixtures, and closets. He wanted a TV room big enough to accommodate a NordicTrack. I told him he could ski in his workroom off the garage. He never did anything else there.

He wanted a skylight over the shower. I could visualize American Airlines flying low to give passengers on the left side of the plane a peek at my body. He said it was against FAA regulations to jeopardize the sight of 180 passengers.

When the contractor suggested an ironing board built into the wall, Bill requested,

"Put a sign on it so Erma will know what it is."

The gestation period of two years was beginning to take its toll on us. We were tired of carrying it around. Every time someone would ask us, "How's the house coming?" we turned our backs and walked out of the room.

Two weeks before Christmas in 1982, we gave birth to a healthy Santa Fe house on a mountaintop in Arizona.

After delivery, the mother was in the kitchen with no running water, no electricity, and no phone surrounded by thirteen packing boxes marked "Miscellaneous."

The daddy of this architectural miracle was watching television, recovering from back surgery.

I looked at Bill lounging in the family room. No one would ever convince me the back surgery was not calculated. He did it on purpose. The heaviest thing he could lift was the remote control.

As I dropped yet another carton of books off, I said to him, "The dog hates it here."

"You don't know that," he said.

"When someone wets on every chair leg in the house he is telling you something."

"Didn't we cut a large hole in the kitchen wall for a doggie door?"

"Two of them. He doesn't like it out there."

"The dog is spoiled," he said. "We ought to find him a new home."

"It's hard turning someone out who bought us a set of shrimp forks for Christmas last year."

"Look, things look bad right now, but it's a beautiful house. I wouldn't change a thing."

"That's because you don't have to walk fifty-six steps to the bathroom four times a night, dear."

"I told you, sweetheart, to take the other bed that's closer to my bathroom."

"Oh sure, and get stuck with your dinky closet. You'd like that, wouldn't you?"

"About as much as I like your idea of the utility room near the family room. There's nothing I like any more than pulsating and spinning when 'Monday Night Football' is on."

"Well, your idea of having a house paved with tile wasn't the greatest idea you ever had. These floors are killing my varicose veins."

"Why didn't you think of that before we sank all those bucks into this stuff?"

"For the same reason you chose all those trees around the doors that give me sinus infections."

I grabbed a dust cloth and clutched it in

my fist and ranted as I lifted it toward the ceiling, "As God is my witness, I will never move again."

"Don't tell me," said Bill. "That's supposed to be a turnip."

"Too much, right?"

"A bit," he said.

The fifties went fast. Probably because we were trying to jam as much into them as we possibly could. When a marriage unloads the children and responsibilities, you have to fill it back up again.

The house *was* like a child that needed maintenance, attention, supervision, and goals. I had a dream that before I died all the lights and all the appliances would work at the same time.

We told everyone it was absolutely, positively, unequivocally the last house we would ever buy.

We lied.

"As Long as He Needs Me"

———— 🌹 ————

In 1985, Bill and I bought a pair of lovebirds at a pet shop in the mall. They were irresistible with their fern-green bodies, their peach faces, and their black eyes watching your every move.

A couple of years later, while passing by their cage, I noted that the female had nearly severed the head of the male with her beak. We immediately put them in separate cages and nursed the male back to health.

Everyone was shocked but me. You burden someone with the name of lovebird and what do you expect—miracles? Just try spending all that time in a cage with old grain breath and see how kissy kissy you are at the

Erma Bombeck

end of the day. First, it's little things like swinging on the ring when your mate is trying to sleep. Then it's dominating the water supply. Even birds can take just so much togetherness. They can't live up to the name.

It's the same with couples. After thirty-six years of marriage there are expectations that must be met. No one ever expects you to leave a room when the other one walks in. The trick is not to take it personally. It doesn't mean you're out of love. It means you have the confidence at this stage to assert your independence.

The idea of separating had been terrifying for us. The simple truth is, we needed one another to function.

My husband wouldn't be alive today if I didn't help him drive. The man owes me big time. He considers me tense and rigid when I drive with him. I think the phrase he used was, "It's like being around a constipated bullfighter." He, on the other hand, drives too fast, tailgates, and doesn't plan for contingencies.

He also passes cars. I do not like to ride with drivers who pass cars. It's a terrible habit. Okay, so maybe the car ahead of you is going 15 miles per hour and you have to follow it for 200 or 300 miles. What's the big hurry?

"As Long as He Needs Me"

He also has another trick that makes me crazy. He makes left-hand turns. With just a little planning, he could go around the block and make a right-hand turn, but no, he has to pull up to an intersection and take a chance that all those cars are going to stop for a red light and let him turn left. It's just too iffy.

Another horrifying truth I discovered was that I needed Bill to finish a sentence. Someone figured out that past the age of thirty-five, the average person loses 100,000 brain cells a day. Quite simply, it means every day of our lives the pilot light diminishes, the elevator stops at fewer floors . . . it takes longer for the pot to boil.

Out of the clear blue sky Bill would ask, "What was the name of Fred MacMurray's housekeeper in *My Three Sons*?"

"If you still have any feeling for me, you won't ask me to do this," I said.

"It was Bill something," he said.

"How about William Frawley?" I asked.

"No, he was the butler on . . . what was that show with the three kids and the guy on *Hardcastle and McCormick*?"

"No, no, he had a beard and Frawley was bald and was—"

"On the Lucy show. What was Ethel's real name?"

Erma Bombeck

"Vivian."

"Blaine?" he asked.

"Vance. What was the original question?"

"I forgot."

Sometimes when we were in a group, we would converse in tandem. The other people wouldn't know who they were talking to.

ERMA: I heard the most amusing story the other day. This fella . . . he used to be our insurance salesman . . . Oh, what's his name? Ben . . . something . . . begins with a B.

BILL: Fred . . . Fred Zwack.

ERMA: That's him. You'd all know him if you saw him. He looks like the movie star . . . You know, Jim Arness in *Gunsmoke*? His brother . . . tall, blond . . .

BILL: Peter Graves.

ERMA: Yes! He was on that show for a long time where your assignment self-destructed . . . "Mission Unbelievable."

BILL: Impossible.

ERMA: Right. Anyway, this dog was in . . . it wasn't a bar exactly . . . You know, the lights twirled around and loud music . . .

BILL: Disco.

ERMA: He was in a disco and a guy came up and offered to buy him a drink. It was a weird concoction.

BILL: Is it important to the story?

ERMA: Yes.

BILL: A California slinger?

ERMA: Beer! It was a beer. And the dog said . . .

As all eyes waited in anticipated relief, I said, "Talk among yourselves; I have to think what the punch line is."

When we noticed this happening, we decided to keep our minds razor sharp by testing them. So each day at 4:30 we lined up on the sofa to watch *Jeopardy*.

It was pitiful. We knew the history answers. (Why shouldn't we? We were there!) But by the time we got the answers out, we were into the six o'clock news.

We had both come to the point where we were taking care of one another whether we wanted to be taken care of or not.

I thought I was capable of reading, but every morning he felt compelled to leap from his bed, take the rubber band off the newspaper, and read it aloud to me like I was sitting on Barbara Bush's lap in a literacy program.

"Listen to this, Erma," he would announce. "Lady, a four-year-old collie, was breathless after a long journey home in Minnesota."

"I'll read it later," I warned.

"Fleeing a forest fire near Tower, she

walked all the way to Duluth. Some would say it's instinct; some would say it's the power of love. The long journey began—"

"Give me a break," I snarled. "I've read Dear Abby three times."

"On Mother's Day the fire raged near the Riesgrafs' cabin."

"Look," I shouted, "I don't care if the dog came home in a cab. Don't read to me!"

When he wasn't reading aloud to me, he was ripping stories out of the paper and taping them to my mirror or hanging them on the refrigerator.

We stayed together for other reasons— not the least being the comfort zone. The small dark corners of our moods, likes, and dislikes had been illuminated and there were few surprises.

We had staked out our territories. He had his "parking spot" in the garage, he occupied the same chair at the dinner table, slept on the same side of the bed no matter where we were, and in church we sat in the same section every Sunday.

At age fifty-seven, we tended to "hang out" with people who had lived through our war, had our same morality, and got tired at the same hour we did.

The idea of turning back the clock, which

had once seemed so exciting and attractive to us, had now turned into a practical approach.

A lot of my friends were paying for new noses and sleeping with surprised looks on their faces from lifts that were pulled tighter than a marine's bedsheet.

I told my friend one day, "Look, I've been thinking over this cosmetic surgery and to tell you the truth, I'm not all that convinced it would be in my best interest."

"Why not?" she said.

"Okay, just suppose I decided to buy a face-lift on credit. It would cost about $4,000 and my monthly payments would run $92.

"With the payments on the house, the car, and the VCR, I'd spend so much time worrying about how to make ends meet, it wouldn't be long until my eyes hung in swags like theater curtains."

"I hear you," she said.

"Now, I have the eyes done for $2,000. The monthly payment on them would run about $74.

"So I'm going to work early and staying late . . . hunched over my typewriter and eventually my chest begins to sag and someone suggests implants."

"I'm ahead of you," she said.

"Right. My new chest would cost $2,700 and my monthly payments would run about $69. By this time I could never leave my desk. I'd have to exercise in order to have liposuction. Now I've got plastic surgery bills that total $11,700 and monthly payments of $319. The more I worry, the more wrinkles return and the body falls like a stone."

"So what are you going to do?" she asked.

"For the moment, lie on my back with my head hung over the side of the bed. It's a moment."

Bill and I were looking at age sixty . . . the age of our grandparents, for God's sake. The age when they supposedly had no body, little mind, and couldn't afford the luxury of buying green bananas.

I passed the lovebirds' cages one day and the male had untwisted the wire that held the door shut with his beak, tapped at it until he could thread his body through it, and escaped. To freedom? Not exactly. He had flown over to the cage of the female where they pecked lovingly at one another through the bars.

Some would call it love. I knew in my heart he just wanted back in to read the newspaper at the bottom of the cage out loud to her.

Metamorphosis

❧

Sitting next to Mother in a pastel room in a funeral home, I felt like I was watching an evening at the Improv with Mike Nichols and Elaine May. God, why was I thinking about that classic skit at a time like this?

ELAINE: Hello there, I'm your grief lady.

MIKE: (crying) I know.

ELAINE: We have a top-of-the-line funeral we could offer for your uncle.

MIKE: That sounds wonderful. What does that include?

ELAINE: We offer a $10,000 casket. Orchids flown in from Hawaii and the Mormon

Erma Bombeck

Tabernacle Choir. Or we have a down-
scale funeral.

MIKE: Which is?

ELAINE: We have Perry Como on record
singing the "Ave Maria." Then we put
your uncle on a public bus and God
knows where they take him.

The caregiver behind the desk was whis-
pering to my mother, "Just a few more questions, Mrs. Harris, and then we're finished.
On the embossed thank-you cards for your
husband, do you want a cross or a rose?"

Mother sighed and looked to me. She
looked so small and helpless.

"Rose," I snapped.

It wasn't his fault. He was a nice man
doing his job. It was me. For the first time, I
felt old. I had been someone's mother, someone's wife, someone's daughter, but never a
matriarch before. The crown weighed heavily
on my head.

Two days later as prayers were said over
my father, I held the hands of my mother, the
hands that had guided mine to a million
patty-cakes. As we rose to leave the chapel, I
steadied and guided her as she had steadied
and guided me on my first pair of roller
skates so I wouldn't fall. I slowed my steps to

walk in cadence with the legs that had lifted me to Banbury Cross.

The metamorphosis had begun.

The trading of roles between a mother and her child has a lot to do with marriage. It affects the way you live, the way you think, and the way you are and are going to be. I have seen some daughters ease into the role reversal with grace. I had to be dragged, screaming all the way.

I had always admired my mother's strength, especially during my father's three-year-long illness. She had done incredible things she never dreamt she could do. She drove in rush hour traffic, learned how to regulate oxygen and fill portable tanks, used a copier in the supermarket, paid bills, and pumped her own gas.

Now she was just plain tired and needed someone to take care of her. Nearly all of my contemporaries had been there.

Some were exhilarated at the prospect of at last becoming wise. The mother who ragged them constantly about using the water left over from the spaghetti to starch their husbands' shirts now needed their daughters' advice on investments.

Some reacted with the fear of having responsibility for yet another human being. It was like giving birth to a child at age sixty. The stamina just wasn't there.

I had a reaction that even surprised me. There was anger. It was too soon for my mother to relinquish her life to me. I was an ingenue in rehearsal still learning my part. I wasn't ready yet for opening night. I wanted her to go on being strong. I wanted her to be in charge of her own life as she had always been. I wanted her . . . I wanted her to be thirty-three years old again.

I didn't want my mother to be eighty-something. What it was really about was that I was looking at the only buffer left between me and my own mortality.

I would have had to be blind not to see the parallel between our grown-child-to-elderly-parent relationship and the mother-to-young-child relationship.

"Wait a minute, Mother, your dress zipper isn't zipped all the way." ("Just a second, Missy, you got dirt on your face.")

"You'd better get to bed early, Mom. You have an early dental appointment." ("Get to sleep up there. You got school tomorrow.")

"I'm chilly in here. Let me get you a sweater." ("You're hot now, but trust me, you're going to need a sweater.")

"If you didn't order so much you wouldn't

need a doggy bag." ("Erma Lou and her big eyes. Clean up your plate!")

One weekend, my cousin Dede and I took our mothers, who are sisters, to Las Vegas. We hailed the cab for them, registered at the hotel and held the key for safekeeping, admonished them not to get lost, and told them three times where we would meet. (We did everything but carry an antenna with a fake flower on it.) We made them go to the restroom when they said they didn't have to go, and while they were in the booth I yelled from outside, "Are you all right in there?"

At that moment, my eyes met Dede's. What was happening to us? "I can't believe I said that," I said.

"What do we think they are doing," she said, "playing in the toilets?"

What we were doing was what we had observed growing up from these two women in the stalls. They had a duty to take care of us and now the duty to take care of them had fallen to us.

And their reactions were the same as ours were when we were the child.

"Mom, this car doesn't move until you find your seat belt." ("She treats me like a baby.")

"Don't get up. Just tell me what you want." ("I'm not an invalid.")

Erma Bombeck

"I cannot believe you thought the oven cleaner was spray starch." ("Lord, I shouldn't have told her. She has that going-to-the-home look.")

Men somehow seem to escape the role-reversal thing. Bill was just the middle man. Mother and I both dumped on him, and being the wisest man in the world, he said nothing. "You have to respect a woman who, at age eighty, takes on a new career: claim filing," he offered.

It's something you don't appreciate until you go through it. One day she fell off a ladder in the garage. ("I told you you would fall, but you wouldn't listen.") As she was lying on her back in the garage, she yelled, "Before you call an ambulance, get my purse and make sure you get the company where I have full coverage."

I got her billfold and have to tell you I have never had more respect for my mother than I did at that moment. It held more medical phone numbers than the yellow pages.

"I don't mind the injury," she said, "but it's all those stupid forms."

I called her for lunch one day a few weeks later and she said, "I can't talk to you. This is my day to copy things."

"What does that mean?" I asked.

"It means I go to the supermarket with a

pocketful of change and use the copying machine to run off extras of all my records to send to people."

"Do you have any idea what you're doing?" I asked.

"Not a clue," she said.

"Are you saying you can't go to lunch?"

"That's what I'm saying. I'm waiting for a call from Medicare, another from Social Security, and one from an insurance company that only pays sixty percent. I have to file with another insurance company for the ambulance and another for the medication.

"Oh, by the way, your father received a letter from a recruiting officer inviting him to join the Navy."

"So, what's the question?"

"Don't they realize how old he would be?"

"Mom, the big issue here is he's dead."

"I know that, but he keeps getting mail. He's even been offered a gold credit card. They say his credit line is very good."

"I'll bet it is."

When I got over the anger of my mother not being thirty-three years old, we began to settle comfortably into the new structure. Slowly, and with the help of Bill, I began to appreciate what it must be like for grand-mothers to relinquish their status.

Erma Bombeck

America does not treat its elderly well. In Europe, my widowed mother would have lived in the house with her daughter or son . . . not as a boarder or an accessory, but as head of the house. She would be respected and listened to until the day she died. Only then would the role of head of the house be handed down to her daughter or daughter-in-law.

Here, the elderly must fend for themselves and be at the mercy of their children. I never wanted my mother to feel like that. She is a nice, vibrant, funny lady, and she deserves better.

Our differences were stunning to the eye. She was country-western; I was Liza Minnelli. She loved soaps; I loved "Jeopardy." I wrote books; she used them for doorstops. I was an introvert. She did twenty minutes in front of the bathroom mirror. I was almost a recluse. She went to the opening of an aspirin bottle. I hated crowds. She could talk to a wall. I liked chocolate. She loved rhubarb.

One day in August, I received a call from Mom. She told me that she had a lump on her breast and they were going to do a biopsy. I checked her in at the hospital and went to her house to wait it out.

I had never seen her house before when there was no one in it. There were always people hanging around the kitchen. The television set was always blaring. The table was usually set.

It was a house I had never lived in. The one I grew up in had unsightly holes in the bedroom walls and adhesive tape permanently embedded on the walls from my posters, and a bed buried beneath clothes and wet towels.

No, this was their dream home. She and my late stepfather had earned it, working right up to retirement in an Ohio factory. This was where they were going to kick back and make withdrawals from lifetime deposits of savings and sacrifices.

I pushed open the bathroom door. You could have performed surgery on the sparkling tiles. The soaps were shaped like hearts.

In the kitchen was a pencil and pad by her Bart Simpson portable phone she received from her grandson last Christmas. I smiled whenever I heard her mumble in the receiver, "Wait a minute. It's not easy talking into someone's fanny."

I straightened a picture on her brag wall in the hallway . . . pictures of her grandchildren at various stages of their lives . . . a warm greeting on a picture of Wayne Newton . . . framed covers of my books. (When someone just happened to ask her if she was my mother, she would answer dryly, "Someone had to do it!")

Before closing the doors on these walls of silence to visit her at the hospital, I remember thinking how often we look, but never see . . . we listen, but never hear . . . we exist, but never feel. We take our relationships for granted. A house is only a place. It has no life of its own. It needs human voices, activity, and laughter to come alive. It needed my mother shoving a picture of an appetizer into the face of a late-arriving guest and saying, "These are the hors d'oeuvres you missed." It needed her talking a mile a minute into Bart Simpson's fanny.

I realized how selfish I had been. Most children are. I had dedicated my life to "pleasing mama." When I was six, the curtains would part between our dining and living room and I would tap dance and sing "On the Good Ship Lollipop" and she would applaud.

When I was the first one in the family to graduate from high school, she applauded.

At the wedding, she kept things in the kitchen moving, and at the birth of the babies, she cleaned my oven and defrosted my refrigerator. She waved from the stands when I was Grand Marshal of the Rose Bowl parade and taped me as I introduced the Pope to the people of Phoenix. She had rejoiced in my successes and comforted me in my failures.

Now, my number-one fan had other priorities. Survival.

I was part of that survival. What if her health was such that we would share the same house? God forbid, the same kitchen?

We had tried it before with disastrous results. Even a Sunday visit turned into a major confrontation.

The simple truth is I cannot share a kitchen with my mother. This wonderful woman who gave me life, nurtured me, shared my ambitions, secrets, and comforted me in despair gives new meaning to the words, "Let me help."

Women are by nature territorial creatures. Early in life we stake out our domains and heaven help anyone who tries to trespass. To me, working in the kitchen is like giving birth. There are just some things you have to do by yourself. Invariably, when I am at a hot stove up to my armpits in stress, my mother joins me. "Ummm, that looks good," she says. "No one makes potato salad better than you, dear. Your dish towels need bleaching. Anything I can help you with?"

Erma Bombeck

"Everything is under control," I say evenly.

"Did you mean for these lumps to boil?" she asks.

"What lumps?"

"It's hard to tell. Is it gravy or what sauce?"

"It's macaroni, Mother."

"What is this meal? A carbohydrate festival? How many starches can you have at one meal? You weren't raised that way."

"Mother, why don't you fix the relish plate?"

"If it will help you. You know your carrots would stay fresher if you left the tops on them. So how do you cut your tomatoes?"

"Mother, they're not 'my' tomatoes and you've been cutting tomatoes for fifty years."

"When I quartered them once, you were upset. You wanted them sliced."

"Whatever. What are you doing to the onions?" I ask.

"Cutting the tops off. Who eats that part anyway?"

"It just makes them look nicer."

"I suppose that's why you took the carry-out chicken out of the bucket and arranged it on the platter. Where's your dill?"

"Don't start. It's in the spice rack somewhere."

"I put them in alphabetical order the last time I was here and now you've messed them up. You're not going to put a little pimento in your potato salad for color?"

"I hate pimentos."

"You never said that when you lived at home."

"You never asked me. Could you put the pickles in a separate dish? They're running all over the tomatoes."

"My feet are sticking to your floor, and you're whining about a little pickle juice on the tomatoes?"

We could never be trusted to be around blunt instruments together.

In the waiting room, I read the same page of a book three times. Somehow, we would both adjust to our new roles. Mothers and daughters had been doing it since the beginning of time. We would do it because we loved one another.

Mother's doctor approached and sat down beside me. He then spoke the most beautiful word in the English language, "Benign."

A few hours later, I eased my mother's arms into a robe and leaned over to put slippers on her feet for the ride home.

"You look worried," she said.

"Why wouldn't I be?" I asked.

She smiled. "I can't die yet. I just bought a case of toilet paper at the Price Club."

Make Me a Grandmother

All anyone talked about were biological clocks. The whiners on TV's "Thirtysomething" chewed it over like a piece of tough meat every week.

They talked openly of artificial insemination, surrogate mothers, and frozen sperm. (Giving new meaning to designer genes.)

I didn't care about any of this. I wanted to be a grandmother and I was teetering between senility and death. My interest span was becoming limited, patience was in short supply, and I was beginning to forget all the cute games and nursery rhymes. I was out of touch with new toys and TV shows for children. In a few years, I'd throw the baby up into the air and forget to catch him.

All my friends had grandchildren. Me? I was as out-of-sync with my contemporaries as I had been in the '50s when they were dropping babies like lottery balls and I was burning candles to Our Lady of Impossible Conception.

I didn't want to labor it or put pressure on my kids. I just called them every day and left a message on their answering machines, "Why are you punishing your mother?"

It wasn't like I was asking for major sacrifices. All I wanted was for them to get married, live in borderline poverty, drag around for nine months with a little nausea and eight pounds of stomach to stuff under a steering wheel, and surrender two weeks of pay to present me with a small bundle I could play patty-cake with and buy cute presents for when we traveled.

I fancied myself as Auntie Mame. There was so much to teach them about life and so little time. I wanted to show my grandson how to bluff his way out of an inside straight. I wanted to take my granddaughter to the mall and dress up like dance hall girls in a saloon and have our pictures taken together in a little booth.

Erma Bombeck

I wanted people to stop me in a super-market and say, "Your baby is beautiful!" and I would fan myself with a pound of bacon and protest, "Oh puleeese, I'm the grandmother."

I probably wanted revenge.

It is a fact of life that your children never appreciate all you've gone through until they've been quarantined with three kids with measles ... during Christmas ... when the washer isn't working ... and neither is your husband.

They have to experience the exhilaration of kids spitting out their gum in their hands ... or washing three small faces with one small handkerchief full of spit ... or having their offspring take their checkbook to school for Show and Tell to have the proper respect for the profession.

Actually, I did lust for the smooth little bodies with breaths that smelled like milk and little heads with the faint aroma of baby powder. I wanted little fingers to grab onto mine like they needed me and little eyes that followed me around the room when I came into it.

I was beyond the point of just talking about it; I was beginning to have dreams of what life would be like with Grandma Bombeck.

Make Me a Grandmother

The dream always started out the same. My son would kick open the door and drag in a hobby horse (taking a large chunk of wood out of the wall) and yell, "Mom! You home? We'd have called first, but we were running late and couldn't get the real sitter. We knew you wouldn't mind watching Christopher for a night."

"You didn't have to bring the rocking horse, dear," I smiled. "You already left the corral and we eat off the space ship stored in the kitchen."

"He wants the hobby horse, Mom. Reach in my pocket. See that list? He has a small cold. Give him a spoonful of the red stuff three times a day and a little white pill just before he goes to bed. The vaporizer is in the bag and all the doctors' numbers. He has to take the pills on a full stomach and he'll spit the syrup in your face, but keep throwing it in until he swallows it."

As he leaves, his brother is coming up the walk with his two children in tow, Velcro Fingers and Terminator II. Within thirty seconds, they have taken the bathroom door off the hinges, clogged up the toilet with a shoe, put meal worm in the refrigerator for their hamster, which is in the middle of the coffee table, crayoned on the fireplace, flooded the patio, and sold me two chances on a pony.

My teenage granddaughter stops by to tell me she wants to move in with us where she'll have more freedom. Besides, my car isn't run often enough and she'll take care of that. It's okay with her mom if it's all right with me. She introduces me to her boyfriend who wears an earring and has a four-letter word on the bumper of his pickup truck.

The baby falls off the hobby horse. Velcro Fingers wants to know if he can keep the wax apple he has already taken a bite out of and Terminator II has drawn a picture of his hand on the wall behind the sofa.

They move on to the piano where they play "Chopsticks" over and over. I threaten to destroy their puppy. The baby wipes its nose on the new slipcovers.

I promise to read them all a story, but they want to sit in the middle of the floor and play poker. They all cheat.

As the teenage grandchild makes a long-distance call that lasts sixty-five minutes before she splits, I try to get up from the floor when one of them comments, "Grandma, you oughta lose those thighs."

I tell everyone it's nap time. They tuck me in and crank up the TV set.

Make Me a Grandmother

I always awake from these dreams in a cold sweat. What am I thinking! This isn't the way grandparenting is. It's a high-level consultant's job. Grandparents criticize when things aren't being done right, exchange wet bottoms for dry ones and crises for fun times. Grandmothers have three major objectives: keep billfold pictures current, buy whatever their grandchildren are selling, and give kids impractical gifts that parents have forbidden them to have.

The reality is the first child to place a baby in my arms that grabs my finger, stuffs its foot in its mouth, and smiles at me when I say, "This is your grandma"—gets it all.

After 60, It's Patch, Patch, Patch!

⚜

Neither of us had talked a lot during dinner.
When we did it was generic bits of observations like, "Did I tell you Mother is getting a tax refund?" or, "*Northern Exposure* really is getting weird, isn't it?"

After the meal, I slipped away from the table and went into the bathroom where I locked the door behind me. Slowly, like a reluctant stripper, I unbuttoned my blouse and removed my bra. For a full minute, I looked at my breasts in the full-length mirror. Tomorrow at noon the left one would be gone. I had cancer and was having a modified radical mastectomy.

What was the matter with me? Two

breasts weren't something I listed on my resume, for crying out loud. It was just a boob . . . a hooter . . . a part of my anatomy that supported a name tag. Nothing more. Here I was acting like a mother saying good-bye to her seven year old before he left for camp!

Who perpetuated the myth that breasts define your sexuality? Was it the anchorperson I heard on TV a week or so ago who teased, "There are ways to help you become a whole woman after a mastectomy. Tune in at ten."

A whole woman? What were we? Appliances that came with a lifetime guarantee? When a part broke down, we were discounted?

Did men keep the myth alive by never asking a flat-chested girl to the prom? Or did women do it to themselves by "stuffing with cotton what God had forgotten?"

If I were really honest with myself, I'd admit that vanity was only a smoke screen to take my mind off the real problem. I was facing a stretch of bad road and didn't know what it was going to do to us.

A serious illness is marriage's unspoken fear. The chances of a couple staying healthy together and dying at the same time are Las Vegas odds. Life is a dance you want to finish on the same beat. And I was the first to stumble. It should have been the other way around. Women are the nurturers. Insurance charts had all but assured us that we would be the ones to dispense care and love.

These aren't easy adjustments for two people who prided themselves on being in control of their own lives. We had a long run playing our respective roles. Now the director was passing out scripts giving us new identities and unfamiliar lines. I brought very little experience to my new character. Four years before, I had written a book on children surviving cancer, *I Want to Grow Up, I Want to Grow Hair, I Want to Go to Boise.* For two years I walked in their fragile world, visiting them at camps, interviewing them, talking to their parents, doctors and friends, reading their poetry and their diaries. I took copious notes. I nodded and smiled and said I understood what they were talking about, but I didn't. I didn't have a clue where they got their strength and what they told themselves when they were deprived of their childhoods.

I was a visitor in their neighborhood of white walls, worried faces, drugs, and needles. At night, I went home to my safe, normal household where my only worry was whether I over-salted the lasagna.

After 60, It's Patch, Patch, Patch!

I tried desperately to recall their voices. What was it that got them through it? Faith, of course. Anger, a little. Resignation, a fair amount. But the word I heard the most was "humor." These kids had gone through hospital wards, doffed wigs from their bald heads, and said, "See what happens when you don't eat your broccoli?" They had put their prosthesis in the back seat of a car to trick burglars into thinking there was someone guarding it. One little boy actually fed part of his medication to a house plant and won second place at the science fair.

They said laughter gave them normalcy, perspective, and hope. That's how Bill and I had handled adversity before. And if it ain't broke, don't fix it.

The surgery went well. The lymph nodes were clean. I was lucky. When I was returned to my room, the surgeon appeared and asked how I was feeling. My throat was raw, I had a roaring headache, and my body felt numb. "Does the term 'road kill' have any meaning for you?" I asked.

He sat on the bed and asked if I had looked at my incision yet.

"Are you crazy?"

"I want you to look at it now," he said gently. "You are not going home and cry alone in the shower. We're going to look at this together."

As he removed the bandage, I discovered I wasn't looking at my incision. I was looking at him to see how he would react, which was stupid. He was a doctor. He was used to grossness. He wasn't my husband. Slowly, my eyes came to rest on my chest and the black stitches halfway across it. It looked like a road map of Kansas with only one major road.

"I want you to go home and show it to your husband."

I thought about it for three days, but I didn't do it. I told myself I wanted to spare Bill the pain and the shock, but deep down inside I was afraid that I would see a look of pity and repugnance.

The voices of the Boise book kids came back to me. This time it was the words of young Ted Kennedy, Jr., who lost his leg to cancer. "People are taught we should look perfect," he said. "I wondered who would ever go out with a kid with one leg." I remember looking at this handsome young man, thinking, "Is he nuts?"

When I finally got the nerve to invite my husband to the unveiling of my surgery, I babbled nonstop. "When the stitches come out and the swelling goes down and the discoloration leaves, it'll be better. And with some exercise, this extra skin will work back into my arm . . ."

You'd have thought I was selling him a secondhand Toyota.

I searched his face carefully for his reaction. There was nothing there but love.

Normally, this is where the movie versions of these stories end and the credits roll by and the audience leaves the theater with smiles on their faces.

The speeches of what a brave person I was were dwindling. The covered dishes were played out. The flowers died. I began to develop a real boob fetish. Whenever I watched television, my eyes rested on cleavages. I tortured myself with *Sports Illustrated*'s swimwear edition. I couldn't get Madonna's nuclear-warheads bras out of my mind.

My days at the beach were over. I couldn't frolic in the sand sporting more rubber than an eighteen-wheeler. I was exhausted from hurting, and I was sick to death of walking my fingers up and down the walls to nowhere. Who was I kidding? I acted like I had just had a wart removed. This was major. I could never go to a Loehmann's dressing room again!

Erma Bombeck

When I took my complaints to my surgeon he said, "It sounds like you're ready for the 'You're alive' speech." Despite the fact he had probably delivered it thousands of times, I was impressed by it. He was right. The reality had just set in. As I left the office, his nurse gave me a manila envelope and said, "This isn't a real prosthesis, but until you get a good one, just slip this into your bra and you'll be more balanced."

In the car as Bill drove me home, I opened the envelope and a small wad of cotton fell out. "My God!" I shouted, "I've got bigger dust balls under my bed than this."

I wasn't the only one who needed to find some lightness in all of this.

One of my readers wrote, "Hey, Erma, when life gives you a bunch of lemons—stuff 'em in your bra."

A friend told how she caught her prosthesis in a file drawer, another how when she leaned over to pick up a bag in the supermarket, her prosthesis fell onto the floor.

The healing process was into its third month when Bill checked into the hospital for an emergency appendectomy. Now he had the Show and Tell experience and it was just as difficult for him as it had been for me.

We did a lot of thinking about scars that

summer . . . emotional and physical. At one time we had looked upon them as disfigurements in an otherwise perfect body. Now they represented detours in a road that spanned the distance between sick and well. They were no longer stigmas, but badges of courage and survival.

We would like to have milked our maladies for more pity, but in August we received an engraved invitation announcing the September wedding of our son to his bride.

Bill said, "I hope we get through this before something else falls off."

1992

The Wedding

Sitting side by side in the airport en route to our son's wedding, I observed that if we were merchandise, we would have been marked down. I was wearing a new device that held my prosthesis in place. It was a wedge of tape that attached to my skin. A fake breast was simply pressed against the Velcro side doing away with the need for a bra.

Bill was wearing a jumpsuit, the kind workers wear to cover their clothing while they clean office buildings or work on garbage trucks or poke around under car hoods.

It was the only piece of apparel that didn't irritate his fresh appendectomy incision.

"I have no idea how I'm going to get into my tuxedo for the wedding," he said.

"What are you saying?" I asked sharply.

"I am saying that I cannot zip my pants without severe pain."

"You are not going to take attention away from the centerpieces by exposing yourself!" I said. "These kids have killed themselves and spent a lot of money planning for a nice wedding."

When he didn't respond I said, "Just wear your cummerbund low and button your jacket."

The preboarding call came for those traveling with small children or needing assistance. Then I felt it. The prosthesis had pulled loose from the Velcro and was sliding down toward my waist. I folded my arms and leaned forward.

"Are you all right?" he said.

"Put my carry-on bag on my lap," I commanded.

"What for?"

"You are going to see one of the quickest bits of magic since Houdini." I put my hand down my blouse, extracted the boob and dropped it in my bag. The entire exercise took five seconds tops.

The rest of the flight went without incident until we landed at LAX. Three people stopped Bill and asked which carousel their luggage was on. They thought he was a baggage handler for America West.

Our son smiled nervously as he exchanged glances with his brother and best man, who stood next to him. Getting married was the first thing he had ever done in his entire life to make me happy.

As the bridegroom's mother, I vowed to wear beige and keep my mouth shut. No one believed me when I said it.

The setting was wonderful . . . a large room in a clubhouse that overlooked the Pacific Ocean. As we awaited the arrival of the bride, I looked at the waves that had rushed in with such excitement only to fizzle out and withdraw in a cloak of foam. They would try again.

The exercise was a lot like marriage. For centuries, couples in a rush of passion had joined hands, locked eyes, and optimistically promised to do impossible things for one another for the rest of their lives.

It seems like a lot of sameness day after day, year after year, but each time the waves roll in, they deposit new life, rearrange the beach, and claim a piece of it before they retreat.

Erma Bombeck

Our marriage had been like that.

Bill and I had forty-three years of high and low tides. On rare occasions, it was a day at the beach—smooth, sunny, calm, and uneventful. Other times, it was stormy and angry, churning up our lives in its wake.

Sometimes we crashed into the shore out of control. Other times we had to be returned to our familiar territory kicking and screaming.

The bride glided down the aisle.

Everyone who stages a wedding believes theirs is different. This one was officiated by a rabbi and a priest, who dispensed their blessings in tandem. That was different.

The sound of all those thirty-something biological clocks in one room, drowning out the orchestra, was different.

The wedding feast consisted of a salad sprinkled with rose petals and a dome-covered platter that revealed a little pale chicken that looked like Rosemary's Baby. That was different.

As I perused the wedding gifts, I couldn't help but wonder if we would have been happier if we had started out with a cappuccino maker. Would I have attracted a richer mate if I had owned my own stereo with laser discs? Maybe if I hadn't panicked at twenty-two, I would have met someone with the sentiment

The Wedding

of my son, who proposed to his bride on Valentine's Day on a moonlit beach in Hawaii and was taking her to Venice for their honeymoon.

It was over in such a short time. One moment we were dancing and visiting and posing for pictures. The next, the long white limousine disappeared with the couple around a winding driveway leading away from the club. I saw glimpses of them through the crowd and heard the shouts of good-byes, but we were too late to wave them off.

Later at the hotel as we readied for bed, my body felt like a lead weight. Bill had just reached over to turn off the bedside lamp when the phone rang. "It's for you," he smiled.

It was our son and new daughter-in-law on the phone together. "We didn't get a chance to say good-bye," they said.

I couldn't believe it. Two young, healthy, beautiful people on their wedding night, sipping champagne and calling his mother! I yelled into the phone, "Get a life!"

I was touched by the call. What a wonderful day it had been.

Two people embarking on a life together in which every day would be filled with surprises and challenges. The only thing they could count on was that their marriage would be unique. There wouldn't be another one in the world exactly like it.

As Bill's familiar snoring broke the silence, I lay in the darkness and wondered if my new daughter-in-law had made a list of things she was going to change about her husband like the one I had made forty-three years ago.

Good luck! I was happy to get a carpet changed every ten years. Not only had none of the bad habits gone away, the list of things to fix had gotten longer.

He was more paranoid than ever about the utilities. Just a couple of weeks ago I found him crawling on his hands and knees in the garage extending a rake from his hand to pull in the paper. I had never seen him do that before.

"What are you doing?" I asked.

"Don't come any closer," he shouted. "If you stand up you'll trigger the sensor light."

"Is that what this is all about?"

"The thing burns for fifteen minutes," he said. "No sense wasting electricity."

Christmases still put us on the brink of separation. I slaved twelve hours over a dinner (that people ate in twelve minutes) and went crazy trying to get everyone to the table while the food was still hot. For over forty years, he had jumped up from the table as our forks were poised in mid-air, shouting, "Don't anyone eat or touch anything until I get a picture." By the time he found the camera, the film, and replaced the batteries, we could have been eating cold cuts.

He could still get a rise out of me by embarking on a vacation and, in a plane at 34,000 feet, turning to me to ask, "Did you unplug the coffeepot?"

As I punched my pillow, a light caught the enameled cigar band that had replaced my wedding ring. It said a lot about our marriage. It said tradition had little meaning for us—it was our marriage and we could run it any way we liked—and that although we may not know where we were going, we never forgot where we had been.

There are no marriage manuals. It's just as well. If there were, no one would get married. It would be like reading a book on how babies are born. They both sound worse than they are. There are no guarantees that marriage will work once you get it home. There are no exchanges or credit for returns. No lifetime batteries. It's a high-risk profession.

We want to believe marriage is harder to

survive now because of the times we live in. But every marriage since the beginning of time has had to contend with the same difficulties. Only the names change.

There's a book in every marriage. I wondered what kind would be written about the wedding we had witnessed tonight. Would it be filled with mystery? Romance? Science fiction? Intrigue? Humor? Would it be a boring tome? Warm and wonderful? So exciting that you couldn't put it down? Or a classic that would be read by generations to come? Would it be a short volume? Or a long one?

My guess was that the contents would be a combination of all of the above . . . where the main characters live one page at a time.

Next to me, Bill stirred and in the darkness I heard him mumble, "Erma? You awake?"

"Yes."

"I was just thinking . . . did I give you the keys to the car when we left Phoenix?"

"I don't remember."

"I know I put them on top of the car when I got the luggage out of the trunk, but I don't remember taking them off. Oh well, don't worry about it. Go back to sleep."

In the darkness I rummaged through the contents of my handbag, dragged the luggage

The Wedding

out of the closet and searched it, and dumped the clothes from the bureau drawers in the middle of my bed. As I rifled through the pockets of our clothes, I found the car keys in the pocket of his blue jumpsuit.

"Bill!" I said, shaking him. "I found your car keys."

He continued to snore.

I wanted to end this book with a wise and wonderful statement on how marriages work. I don't have a clue.